CHANGE MANAGEMENT IN CIVIL SOCIETY ORGANISATIONS

Change Management in Civil Society Organisations

S. Hanuman Kennedy

P. Krishna Moorthy

AKANSHA PUBLISHING HOUSE
NEW DELHI • GUWAHATI • VISAKHAPATNAM

AKANSHA PUBLISHING HOUSE
4649-B/21, Ansari Road
Daryaganj, New Delhi-110002
Phones: 23268193, 09435116718
Email: ektabooks@yahoo.com
visit us: www.akanshapublishinghouse.com

Change Management in Civil Society Organisations

First Published 2011

ISBN 978-81-8370-268-3

PRINTED IN INDIA

Published by Akansha Publishing House, New Delhi-110002 and printed at Harmain Offset Press, Delhi.

Contents

Acknowledgements

I acknowledge with deep sense of reverence the divine power bestowed on me by my beloved Master Pujyasri Pardhasaradhi Rajagopalachariji, who made all things in my life possible, including this.

My parents Sri S. Prasasd Rao and Smt S. Karuna Devi have been a constant source of support right from day one of my life till today and I acknowledge their sacrifices with a sense of gratitude and love for all they have done through the thick and thin in my life.

Dr A. Krishna Kumari, my wife, has been at my back throughout this work as a constant source of persuasion and drive and I acknowledge with immense love the affectionate support provided by her, but for which this thesis would not have seen the light of the day.

I Acknowledge with great respect the constant encouragement and cooperation extended by Prof B. Anitha Kumar, SKIM, SK University, who has accepted to be my Research supervisor and guided me all through my academic work. I thank her with gratitude and sincerity.

My special thanks are due to Prof. Ramakrishna Reddy, Head of the Department, SKIM, S K University for his overwhelming support and cooperation all through .

I also thank Prof V V N Rajendra Prasad, Prof CR Visveswara Rao , Vice Chancellor , Vikrama Simhapuri University, Nellore,AP. Prof YV Ramanaiah, Prof K. Ravindra Reddy, Prof P Indira of Dept of Zoology, S K University, Anantapur, for all their good wishes and cooperation.

I acknowledge with affection and love the contribution of my brother Dr Srinivasa Rao, Associate Professor, Jawaharlal Nehru

University, My sisters Sitha Latha, Lalitha Devi, Brothers-in-law Mr. Rama Venkata Rayalu, Mr. Radha Krishna, my sister-in-law Mrs. Vasudha.

I am delighted to acknowledge the involvement, enthusiasm and affection shown by my son Master S. Pardhu Nihar, whose little hands were busy always to help me out during the course of completion of this work.

I humbly acknowledge the publishers of 'SEARCH BULLETIN' and other books and material developed, especially on NGO Management and Training. My special thanks are due for the Executive Director F. Stephen of SEARCH and Mr. Prasad Bandari, from whom the author has drawn inspiration and material.

Authors

Preface

Change is a continuous process in all forms of life including human beings. Changes take place in all dimensions of life: individual, family, community, nation, food, clothing, shelter, transport, communication, values, ideology, systems of governance, sex relations, religious belifes, education and so on. The basic influencing factors of change are economic, technological and demographic. In respect to the economic field, changes take place in the field of agriculture,industry, services, trade and commerce. The predominant change is caused by influence of science and technology embracing several aspects of human life. Similarly, demography has influenced changes in terms of fluctuations in population, migrations and cultural contact. Ideological, political, religious, social, ethnic and racial factors have brought in changes. Individual leadership in the areas of religious and politics has also brought about considerable changes. Changes would take place internally as well as externally. We may think of dimensions of change, rate of change and the diffusion of innovations.

Change management is the process of developing a planned approach to change in an organization. Typically the objective is to maximize the collective efforts of all people involved in the change. Change management can be either reactive, in which case management is responding to changes in the macro environment (that is, the source of the change is external), or proactive, in which case management is initiating the change in order to achieve a desired goal (that is, the source of the change is internal). Change management can be conducted on a continuous basis, on a regular schedule (such as an annual review), or when deemed necessary on a program-by-program basis. Change management can be approached from a number of angles and applied to numerous organizational processes. Its most common uses are in organizational development, information technology management, strategic management, and process management. To be effective, change management should be multi-disciplinary, touching all aspects of the organization. However, at its core, change management is primarily a human resource management issue. This is because implementing new procedures, technologies, and overcoming resistance to change are fundamentally "people issues".

Civil society inhabits the area between individuals (or families) and the state, and is made up of associational groupings of all sorts. In its widest sense, civil society would range from political parties on the more public side of this terrain over to business corporations on the more private side and it would include groups aiming to influence the formation and implementation of public policy as well as groups that have no concern for the public domain at all.

The characteristic institution of civil society to what we may call a 'civil society organisation' (CSO), which can be defined as CSO, that has as one of its primary purposes influencing public policy. Thus while all NGOs are CSOs, by no means all CSOs are also NGOs. In most Third World systems, only a portion of the total society is included within the total universe of CSOs, and only a portion of the NGOs are also CSOs. A purely service-oriented CSO (say, in the health by the same token a CSO could become an NGO if it dropped its advocacy activities to concentrate solely on service delivery.

Change management in civil society organisations is less explored area so far. This book is an endeavour in direction of assessing management of change in CSOs. Based on empirical research findings the information is gathered under the following chapters:

1. Human Resources and Change Management Evolving with the Times;

2. Evolution of Civil Society Organisations;
3. Human Resources Management and Change Management Practices in Civil Society Organizations;
4. Case study of Deccan Development Society (DDS) The Charter of DDS;
5. Case Study of MV Foundation; and
6. Findings, Conclusions and Recommendations.

Hopefully, the contents will enlighten and delight one and all concerned.

We express our gratitude to our mentors, colleagues and friends for their constant inspiration, moral support, able guidance and assistance while working on this project. We are also grateful to our respondents for their cooperation in successfully conducting this research based study.

Finally, we are thankful to Mr. M.P. Misra, Akansha Publishing House, New Delhi for bringing out this book elegantly in the present shape.

Authors

1

Human Resources and Change Management Evolving with the Times

"Behaviour of individual employees and teams influence the overall culture of the organization, and can strengthen or dilute its core values."

The recent global economic slowdown and its impact on the Indian software industry, provides us with an opportunity to review the state of the Human Resources (HR) function in a highly people-intensive business. Looking back, one can clearly distinguish two phases of evolution in the HR function. The first phase, which was dominated by the extraordinary decade-long growth in the Indian industry, the HR function was primarily driven by the need to bridge the vast demand-supply gap of skilled software resources. This was accentuated by very high attrition rates, sometimes reaching as high as 40% per annum! In these circumstances, it was natural that the recruitment aspect of HR was in the forefront. People-development and team-building initiatives were not successful in this uncertain environment, where there was a constant churn out of people. In retrospect, this phase neither helped the organisation nor the people, as it hampered the steady growth of knowledge and skills technical, behavioural as well as managerial.

Today, high attrition rates have become history (hopefully forever)! This has been driven by the significantly reduced demand-supply gap, as well as a willingness of employees to build and invest in a relationship in their existing

Fig 1. 1: Model of HRD

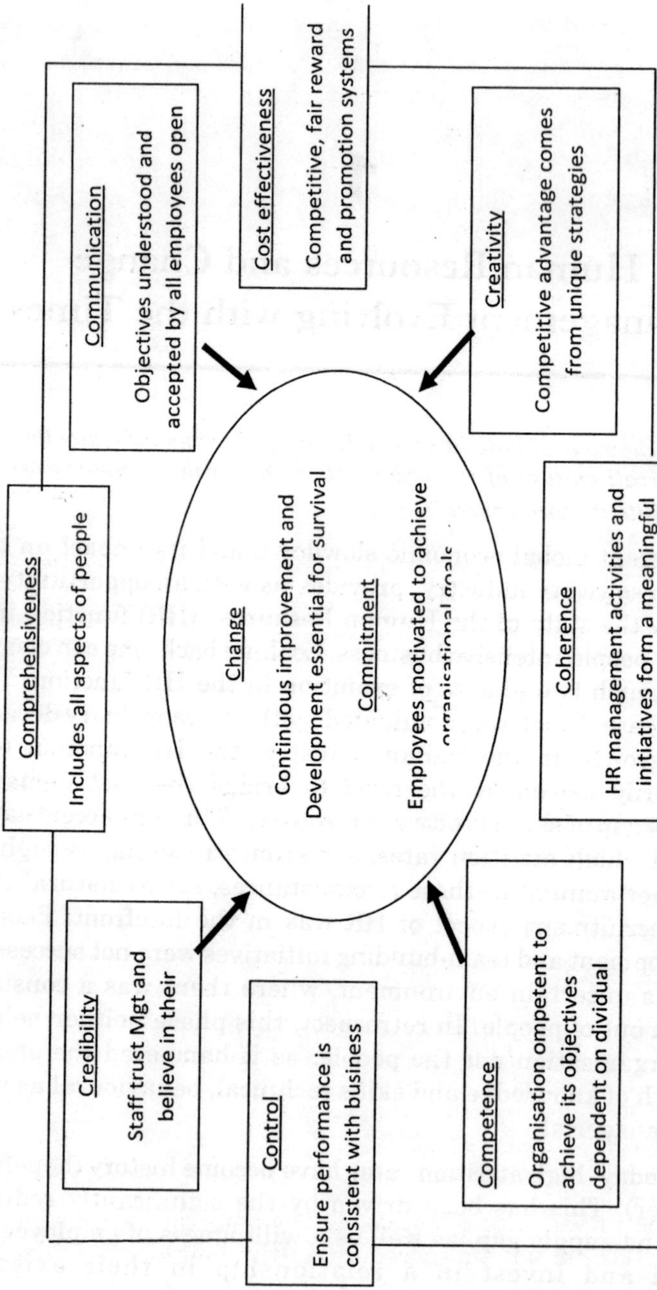

Source: Price, A (1997) –Human Resource Management in a Business context. UK International, Thomas Business Press.

organisations. These days professionals are reviewing their career growth within their organisations and settling for stability instead of frequent job changes. This has become possible with several organisations in India offering much more exciting opportunities coupled with increasing doubts about insecurity of overseas jobs. Aided by this relatively stable people situation, HR has entered a new phase in the Indian software industry. HR in the industry needs to embrace strategies to sustain stability, develop people and improve productivity. (Rao, MVG, 1991) In this dynamic scenario HR practices have been changing and changed to a maximum extent which is a part of change management. Change management and HR functions will go together since change management is a continuous process through human resources management. In this scenario a lot of steps to be taken to enhance the skills of the employees and change them to meet the requirements of day to day happenings. As a part of that now we are looking the model of T&M in the context of HR.

The Figure 1.1 depicts a comprehensive model of T & M in the context of HR Management (Price, 1997).

Strategies to Enhance Employee Skills

To begin with let us look at the performance evaluation system. There is a great need to ensure that it covers every aspect of people development with a strong emphasis on behavioral traits such as:

- Teamwork
- Conflict resolution
- Responsiveness
- Sharing of knowledge and best practices.

It is worth noting that the behaviour of individual employees and teams influence the overall culture of the organisation, and can strengthen or dilute its core values.

The importance of assessing the behavioural patterns of individual employees increases as the employee climbs the career ladder. Once a person attains a people management level there is a need to critically evaluate the individual's behavioral traits.

Performance Evaluation

While we always identify areas of growth and high performers in the organisation, one must be conscious of those people who need improvement. Strategic plans must be in place to enhance the performance level of employees, which are below par. This may not just be due to skills mismatch. Many a time, the concerned person may not integrate well with the organisation's culture, or simply not fit into the team; last but not the least, the employee could be a perpetual poor performer. Even when performance evaluation systems adequately cover the above aspects, the gaps need to be constantly identified and bridged.

Rewards and Recognition

Yet another critical HR tool is -rewards and recognition. They are an important method of keeping employees focused on their long-term career goals. However, reward systems must undergo changes to be relevant and keep pace with the dynamism of people. They need to be exciting for people and have a substantial, positive impact on the organisation's culture. Another important factor that will work to the advantage of the people and the organisation is the nurturing of a unique culture that can bond, attract and retain talent. With people becoming more loyal to their organisations, there is a strong need to build and sustain people bonding with them. Various social, emotional and psychological factors that help in creating a community and a sense of belonging need to be addressed.

Knowledge Management

KM can be a key tool to facilitate bonding. The concept of sharing knowledge and providing "learning windows" apart from the normal training and skill enhancement programmes will go a long way in creating a unique culture in an organisation developing "people through people".

Empowerment

Increasing empowerment and encouraging employees to think, sharing ideas and providing freedom of enterprise can sustain retention of high performers.

Best Practices

Nurturing and developing unique organisational standards like Knowledge Development can contribute towards building its culture that will be a clear "competitive and strategic advantage". Today the most of the industries are in a state of flux, where fast changing business dynamics have transcended cultural and geographical boundaries. In this scenario, organisations must be alert and be in a position to anticipate change and develop strategies to counter change. Being pro-active and developing ownership at all organisational levels must be the new buzzwords of HR. It needs to nurture people who can adapt to changes in the organisation structure, forms of work and the nature of work itself.

In conclusion, the HR mandate in all sectors of industry needs to shift from the numbers game to a concept that encompasses change management, managing people empowerment, career enrichment and energising people towards long-term career goals by creating and sustaining a strong "spirit of enterprise" with a major thrust on innovation.

Human Resource Management and Change

Most authors agree on the drivers for change. Globalization will require seeing and acting beyond local boundaries. Technology will make information more accessible and join people together electronically in ways that can impact organisations and work relationships. A more *knowledge-based work force* will make many employees into volunteers because they could choose to work elsewhere for equal or more money, so they work in an organisation by choice, not by obligation. Turning worker knowledge into productivity and leveraging *intellectual capital* will become work force challenges for future. *Redefining firm performance* away from merely cutting cost to profitable growth also will require change.

Change is a continuous process in all forms of life including human beings. Changes take place in all dimensions of life: individual, family, community, nation, food, clothing, shelter, transport, communication, values, ideology, systems of governance, sex relations, religious belifes, education and so on. The basic influencing factors of change are economic, technological and demographic. In respect to the economic field, changes take place in the field of agriculture,industry, services, trade and commerce. The predominant change is caused by influence of science and technology embracing several aspects of human life. Similarly, demography has influenced changes in terms of fluctuations in population, migrations and cultural contact. Ideological, political, religious, social, ethnic and racial factors have brought in changes. Individual leadership in the areas of religious and politics has also brought about considerable changes. Changes would take place internally as well as externally. We may think of dimensions of change, rate of change and the diffusion of innovations.

Changes also take place as a result of evolution and revolution. A particular change may be progressive or regressive; it may be planned or unplanned. Other global kind of factors which bring changes are demographic and climatic influence and the ways of life of people. There are several theories propounding the causes and ramifications of changes in different walks of life and in different areas. Changes take place in material, cultural, physical, environment, standard of living and interpersonal relations. Wars and colonization have brought in tremendous changes in the life of people.

Some changes are sought after whereas some changes are resisted. This resistance is at the individual as well as community level. In general, you can think of barriers and stimulants to change which may be called cultural, sociological and psychological. While the cultural resistance is in respect to values and traditions, the sociological resistance relates to fear of unknown, ignorance, lack of self confidence and fear of threat to the present status. Throughout history, on the one hand, there have been forces trying to introduce changes and on the other in many fields a continous conflict between these two forces: one trying to improve on the existing system and the other trying to maintain the status quo. Despite such resistance changes have taken place in all dimensions of life. The canvas of change is so vast, touching every aspect of life. Some are progressive and some regressive.

Knowing the pace and unpredictability of change does not mean that firms have learned to manage change. Change redefines risk. In a low change world, reducing risk means getting more of the right answer before taking action. In a world of high amounts of change, reducing risk means acting without full answers but having the capacity to adjust midstream. Agility becomes more important than accuracy in reducing risk. HR professionals cannot assume that they will design the "perfect" program. They must learn to quickly design thoughtful programs, to act on those programs, then to learn and adjust.

Change comes at two levels. First, fundamental change means changing culture or identity. Firms which have for decades had an identity may find that their traditional culture fails to create current customer value; Fundamental culture change will probably affect almost every firm from government agencies learning to become more responsive and service oriented to universities learning to serve students of all ages and across many geographies to airlines mastering customer loyalty.

Second, capacity for change means responding quickly to that which is occurring around us. Reducing the cycle time for completion of business initiatives becomes the requirement and demand for HR professionals. Making things happen more quickly, but still better, is an outcome of change. It can be concluded that the workplace and workforce of tomorrow will be different from that of today, that change outside HR will require change within HR, and that HR is at a crossroads in its ability to deal with this change. (Rao T.V.,1990) Change management is a part of HR. Now we look into the change management and its effect in organizations.

Change Management and Its Importance

Managing change is probably the single most important issue today for all those who have undertaken the difficult task of managing organizations. Technological changes and increased global competition caused by liberalization and deregulation have placed greater demands on organizations to be flexible, responsive and efficient. Around the world, organizations big and small face the inevitable prospect of change.

Organisational change comes in many forms. Organisations may grow bigger, they may become better without becoming begger, they may shrink and become smaller or they may even die. Given the various manifestations of change, it is not suprising that it evokes a myriad of emotions. Some find the propect and experience of change exciting, challenging and fulfilling. Others find it daunting, stressful and unpleasant. It can cause both hope and despair. Managing change involves simultaneously managing resources, processes and emotions. This is what makes change a complicated and challenging task.(V. Nilakant, S.Ramnarayan,1998)

Change will not disappear or dissipate. Technology, civilizations and creative thought will maintain their ever accelerating drive onwards. Managers, and the enterprises they serve, be they public or private, service or manufacturing, will continue to be judged upon their ability to effectively and efficiently manage change. Unfotunately for the managers of the early twenty-first century, their ability to handle complex change situations will be judged over decreasing time scales.

The pace of change has increased dramatically; manking wandered the planet on foot for centuries before the invention of the whell and its subsequent 'technological convergence' with the ox and horse. In one 'short' century a man has waled on the moon; satellites orbit the Earth; the combustion engine has dominated transport and some would say society; robots are a reality and state of the art manufacturing facilities resemble scences from science fiction; your neighbout or competitor, technologicially speaking, could be on the other side of the planet; and bio-technology is the science of the future. The world may not be spinning faster but mankind certainly is!

Business and managers are now faced with hightly dynamic and ever more complex operating environments. Technologies and products, along with the industries they support and serve, are converging. Is the media company in broadcasting, or telecommunications, or data processing, or indeed all of them? Is the supermarket chain in general retail, or is it a provider of financial services? Is the television merely a receiving device for broadcast messages or is it part of an integrated multi-media communications package? Is the airline a provider of transport or the seller of wines, spirits and fancy goods, or the agent for car hire and accommodation?

As industries and products converge, along with the markets they serve, there is a growing realization that a holistic approach to the marking of goods and services is required, thus simplifying the purchasing decision. Strategic alliance, designed to maximize the 'added value' throught a supply chain, while seeking to minimize costs of supply, are fast becoming the competitive weapon of the future. Control and exploitation of the supply chain make good commercial sense in fiercely competitive global markets. The packaging of what were once siscrete products(or services) into what are effectively ' consumer solutions' will continue for the foreseeable future.

The Imperative of Change

Any organization that ignores change does so at its own peril. One might suggest that for many the peril would come sooner rather than later. To survive and prosper organizations must adopt strategies that realistically reflect their ability to manage multiple future scenarios. Drucker, for example argues that: 'Increasingly, a winning strategy will require information about events and conditions outside the institution...only with this information can a business...prepare for new changes and challenges arising from sudden shifts in the world economy and in the nature and content of knowledge itself' (1997: 20-4).

The Impact of Change

What makes an organization want to change? There are a number of specific, even obvious factors which will necessitate movement from the status quo. The most obvious of these relate to changes in the external environment which trigger reaction. An example of this in the last couple of years is the move by car manufacturers and petroleum organizations towards the provision of more environmentally friendly forms of 'produce'. Pettigrew's(1985) analysis of change at ICI attempted to identify what precipitates change. He pointed out that there were no clear beginnings and ends to strategic change. Environmental disturbances were seen as the main precipitating factor, but he also believed that these were not the sole causes of or explanations of change.

To attribute change entirely to the environment would be a denial of extreme magnitude. This would imply that organizations were merely 'bobbing about' on a turbulent sea of change, unable to influence or exercise direction. This is clearly not the case. Pettigrew(1985) went on to argue that changes within an organization take place in response both to business and economic events and to processes of management perception, choice and action. Managers in this sense see events taking place that, to them, signal the need for change. They also perceive the internal contest of change as it relates to structure, culture, systems of power and control. This gives them further clues about whether it is worth trying to introduce change. But what causes change? What factors need to be considered when we look for the causal effects which run from A to B in an organization?

We would like you to think of changes that have occurred in your organization over the last year. How often were these changes the reaction to events that occurred outside your organization? For example, can you cited examples linked to your company's response to:

- Changes in technology used
- Changes in customer expectations or tastes
- Changes as a result of competition
- Changes as a result of government legislation
- Changes as a result of alterations in the economy, at home or abroad
- Changes in communications media
- Changes in society's value systems
- Changes in the supply chain
- Changes in the distribution chain?

Internal changes can be seen as responses or reactions to the outside world which are regarded as external triggers. There are also a large number of factors which lead to what are termed internal triggers for change. Organization redesigns to fit a new product line or new marketing strategy are typical examples, as are changes in job responsibilities to fit new organizational structures.

The final cause of change in organizations is where the organization tries to be ahead of change by being proactive. For example, where the organization tries to anticipate problems in the marketplace or negate the impact of worldwide

Fig 1.2: Key Roles in Sequential Process of Organisational Change

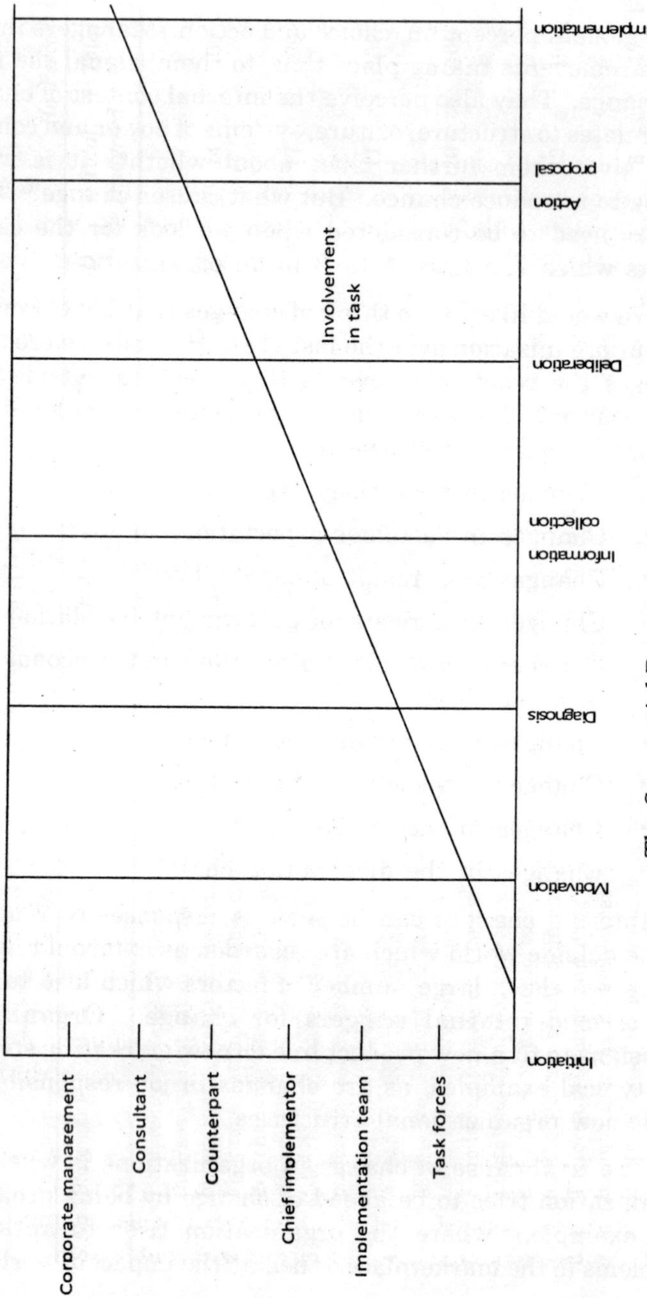

The Sequential Process

Source : ***Introduction to Ever Changing Organisations*, Gerald R.Peters and Doyle W.Young, 1999, SL Lucie Press New York**

recession on its own business, proactive change is taking place (Buchanan and Huczynski, 1997: 461).

Change and Transition Management

If the concept of change can be examined from an internal, external or proactive set of viewpoints, then the response of managers has to be equally as widespread. Buchanan and McCalman(1989) suggest that this requires a framework of 'perpetual transition management'. Following from Lawler's(1986) concept of the lack of a visionary end state, what appears to be required is the ability within managers to deal with constant change. This transition management model, although specifically related to large-scale organizational change, has some interesting insights into what triggers change in organizations, and how they respond. It suggests that four interlocking management processes must take place both to implement and sustain major organizational changes. These processes operate at different levels, and may involve different actors in the organizational hierarchy. The four layers are:

- *Trigger layer*: Concerning the identification of needs and opening for major change deliberately formulated in the form of opportunities rather than threats or crises.
- *Vision layer*: Establishing the future development of the organization by articulating a vision and communicating this effectively in terms of where the organization is heading.
- *Conversion layer*: Setting out to mobilize support in the organization for the new vision as the most appropriate method for dealing with the triggers or change.
- *Maintenance and renewal layer*: Identifying ways in which changes are sustained and enhanced through alterations in attitudes, values and behaviours, and regression back to tradition is avoided.

Transition management suggests that organizations have to plan for, divert resources to, and implement four sets of interlocking processes. These are designed to implement, to sustain, and to build on change and its achievements in an attempt to address the issues associated with change over time. The argument here is that these layers – trigger, vision, conversion, and maintenance and renewal - are necessary processes that occur in change management. The respective emphasis and priority attached to each of them will alter over time, but recognition of their existence goes a long way in determining the management action needed. (Robert A.Paton, James McCalman-2000)

Change management is the process of developing a planned approach to change in an organization. Typically the objective is to maximize the collective efforts of all people involved in the change. Change management can be either reactive, in which case management is responding to changes in the macro environment (that is, the source of the change is external), or proactive, in which case management is initiating the change in order to achieve a desired goal (that is, the source of the change is internal). Change management can be conducted on a continuous basis, on a regular schedule (such as an annual review), or when deemed necessary on a program-by-program basis. Change management can be approached from a number of angles and applied to numerous organizational processes. Its most common uses are in organizational development, information technology management, strategic management, and process management. To be effective, change management should be multi-disciplinary, touching all aspects of the organization. However, at its core, change management is primarily a human resource management issue. This is because implementing new procedures, technologies, and overcoming resistance to change are fundamentally "people issues".

Introducing the Concept of Change

Since all the CSOs deal with communities, the workforce

should also be trained in change management. They should be trained in what change is? How change occurs so that they can manage it effectively. In order to ensure effective development, the change-agent has to introduce the community concerned to the idea and concept of change. They are to be explained the 'why' and 'what' of the transformation that has been proposed to be brought about. The people are to be explained why the change is needed, why some old ideas are to be reformed or given up? What actually are the ideas that are to be given up? What ideas and institutions in the traditional culture inhibit change and how new developments are going to help them?

In order to create an awareness, the change-agent must: (i) reiterate the positive effects of changes, (ii) emphasise on the negative aspects, and (iii) compare the new ones with the old.

Strategy of Change

Techniques

The change initiated follows a course where the ideas and tools are amalgamated harmoniously. Systematic reinforcement of values will not yield desired results unless tools befitting the organisation are employed. Innovation of tools requires an understanding of the socio-economic and political dynamics of the organisation. The forces that interact with the organisation value pattern are multifarious. They effect each other or a number of factors. Therefore, the external and internal forces interacting at all levels of the organisation are to be completely understood by the change-agent for developing tools and strategy.

The direction of change must be patiently watched. The organisation should be allowed to take time to internalize the values. This is time-consuming as there is a feeling of insecurity in dislodging the old and internalizing the new. This sense must be perceived. Therefore, in order to integrate the organisation with the new value patterns, the change-agent must allow enough time. Gradual change is lasting and follows complete integration.

This can be achieved easily if the change-agent is perceived one among the group who has sincere desire for transformation. A feeling of alienation towards the agent of change and the techniques will create disintegration.

After categorising the existing and expected values, the change-agent has to act as follows:

1. Discover the socialization process and study the ways of value transmission by all members of the organistion.
2. Discover how these values are carried over the socio-economic and political structure of the society.
3. Discover areas where change can be speedier and effective.
4. Authenticate assumed aspects of the value system by constant reflection, discussion, communication and contact.
5. Find out ways of conflict resolution and management and how this can be used to achieve the expected goal.
6. Locate persons with commitment in the organisation and enlist their support, realize their experience and activity for achieving the expected goal.

Human beings are receptible to change only when the change is supported by the external environment. When this is possible, positive gains will flow from the new values and people will support the change. But this will be a gradual process. It will be judged to be effective if it penetrates the whole community. The presence of supportive groups in the organisation will facilitate transformation. Effective mobilization, creation of awareness, organisation and social action will lead to achievement of desired goal if the change-agent has commitment and sincerity of purpose.(Nilakanth.V and Ramnarayan S, 1998)

Organizational Change

Organisational change is a complex phenomenon and has several dimensions.

The Sequential Process

There have been several models of the process of organisational change. All these models envisage change as a continuous process involving several stages. The following eight stages are proposed as framework. (See figure 1.3)

1. *Initiation:* Initiation is the stage of vocalization of the need for change. Organisational change starts when someone the level of the corporate management where the concern for some dimension of organisational functioning is shared and discussed. The idea may be mooted at the level of the corporate management, at times based on observations or recommendations by some other level of the organisation, and sometimes as a result of discussion at the level of the corporate management. This usually leads to the hiring of a consultant from outside, or discussion with the appropriate set of people within the organisation.
2. *Motivation:* Motivation is the state of the involvement of people in detailed thinking about the proposed change. At this stage both the corporate management and the expert who helps in the organisational change take necessary steps to involve a larger section of the organisation in thinking about the various dimensions of the change process.
3. *Diagnosis:* Diagnosis is an attempt to search for the main cause of the symptoms encountered.
4. *Information Collection:* At this stage detailed information is collected on the dimension indicated by the diagnosis. Based on the diagnosis necessary information is collected.
5. *Deliberation:* The deliberation stage is concerned with evaluating various alternatives generated for change.

Fig 1.3 : The Model of Implementation of Change in an Organisation

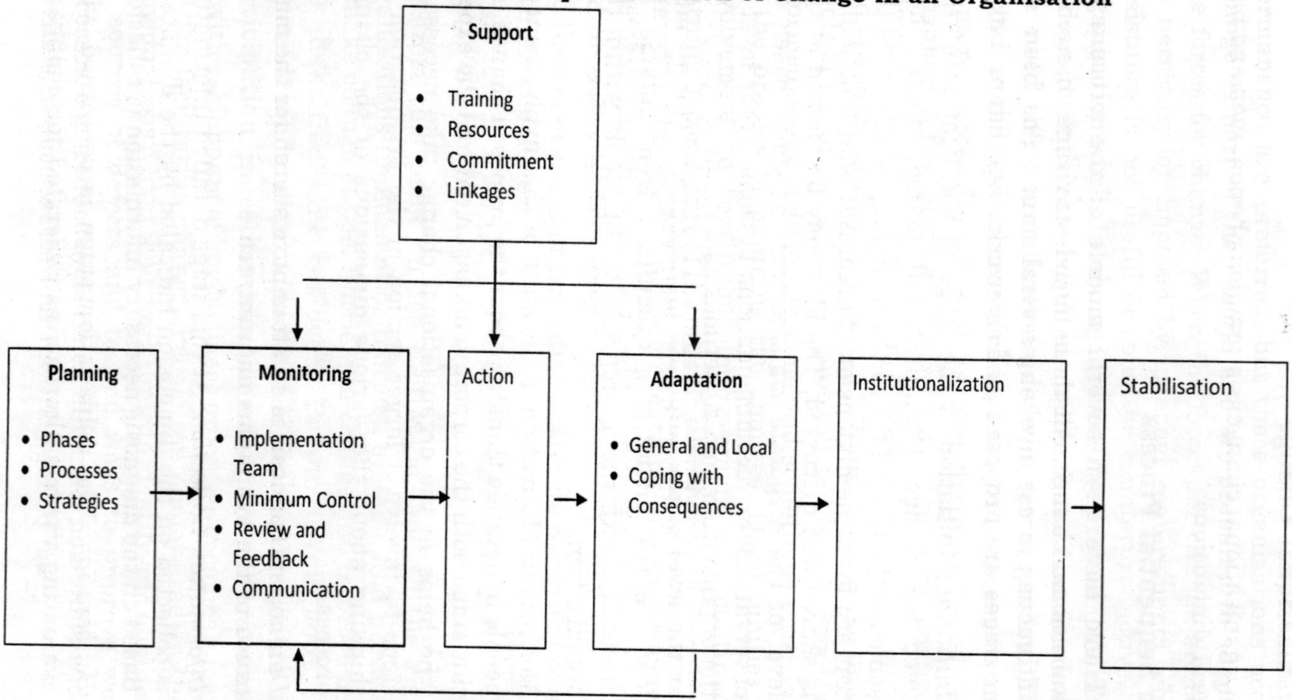

Source : "Managing Change through OD" in T.V.Rao,et.all and Chandra Sekhar.S(1989)

6. *Action Proposal:* This is the stage of framing up an action proposal.
7. *Implementation:* Implementation is concerned with translating the proposal into action.
8. *Stabilisation:* Stabilisation is the stage of internalizing change and making it a part of the organisation's normal life. The various stages in the process of organisational change may be useful to pay attention to the process in the beginning much more and this will help to pay less attention to the process as the organisational change proceeds further. Later much more attention can be given to the task. (Chandrasekhar.S, 1989)

Dealing with Consequences of Changes

A change being an alien element, causes disturbance. When a change is introduced in an organisation, it may produce some threat for some people. Such threats are more imaginary than real; it may also produce some immediate "negative" results. The organisation has to deal with such consequences. If attention is not paid to such consequences, the symptoms may accumulate and may contribute to the rejection of change. The model of implementation of change in an organisation is diagrammatically represented in Fig 1.4.

It has been reported in the change efforts of job enrichment and work redesign that immediately after the change is introduced in an organisation there is a fall in production. In work redesigning efforts, the dissatisfaction of the supervisory staff increases gradually, when they perceive that their roles are becoming redundant. Unless the change programme does something about the dissatisfaction of the supervisory staff (e.g., redesigning their roles, involving them in some critical decisions, etc.), the change may not succeed.

Support

Support of various kinds will be required for the

Fig. 1.4: The Ever Changing Organisation

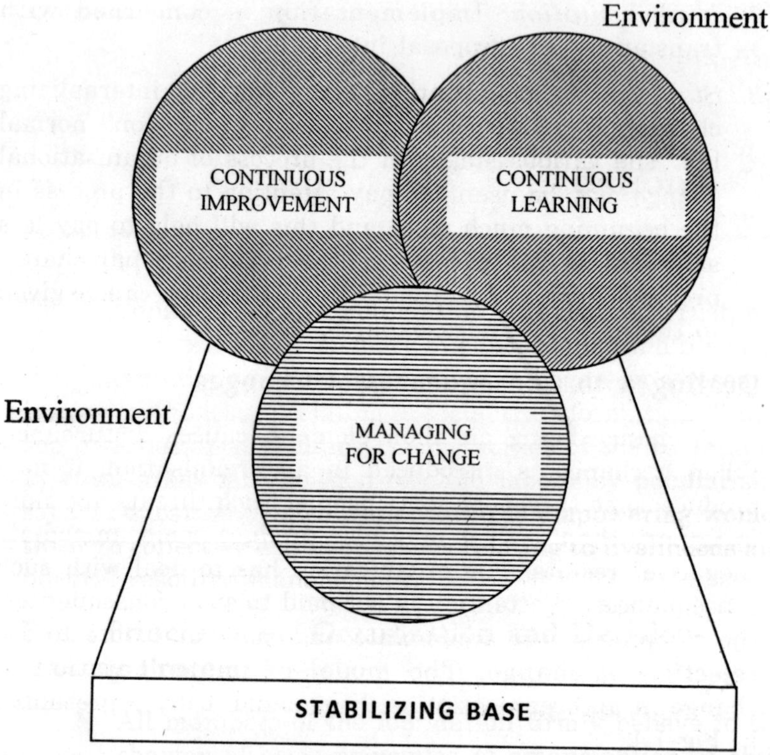

Model of the Ever-Changing Organisation as a system. Key Components are the external environment, a Stabilizing base, and the organisation's managing FOR change, continuous improvement and continuous learning processes.

ORIENTATION OF CHANGE CONTINUUM

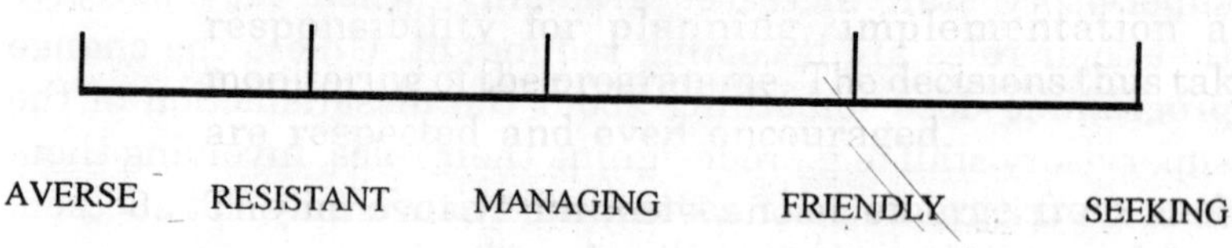

implementation of a programme. The main support comes from administrative and managerial groups. Some main dimensions of support are suggested as follows:

Training

New skills are needed for the implementation of a programme. It is necessary to provide training for such skills. This may include some process skills such as, collaboration, openness, problem solving, decision making, etc. Or, these may be specific technical and work-oriented skills like the skills of planning and using information and collecting information for specific purposes.

Resources

Implementation would require support in terms of various types of resources such as, manpower, financial, and material resources, by people who are implementing the programmes. The implementation team provides such support by finding out what is needed from time to time. Resource support may be needed for all the three aspects—for monitoring, for implementing the action, and for bringing about some modifications and adaptations.

Top Management Commitment

A critical dimension of support is the top management support. The involvement of the top management may be necessary. This may come about if enough signals are given by the top management, that they consider the change as important, that they are interested in its implementation, and they themselves are involved in the change.

Linkages

Support may also be required in terms of building linkages both with external experts and with various other agencies and internal departments and groups who may provide necessary help in the implementation of the programme.

While the programme may officially be the responsibility of one group, it should be the responsibility of the whole organisation to implement it.

Dealing with Resistance to Change

An organisation has to deal with resistance to change. There may be several reasons for resistance to change. If these reasons are understood, effective steps can be taken to reduce resistance. Most steps can be of preventive nature, reducing resistance to a great extent. Some action can be taken when resistance is experienced. We present below some ideas about dealing with resistance to change. Table 1.1 summarizes the sources of resistances and the steps that can be taken to deal with such resistance.

Perceived peripherality of change: If the employees perceive that the change being introduced in the organisation is not critical for them or their units, they are likely to resist such a change. Implementation of change can be effective if the change introduced is seen as critical and useful. This can be achieved by involving the concerned managers in the diagnosis of the issues or problems, so that they can appreciate the need for change. Their attitude to the innovation introduced will then be positive.

Perception of imposition: Similarly, if the managers in an organisation see the change as being imposed by the corporate or the head office, they are likely to resist the change. Such resistance can be reduced by involving them in the introduction of change at several stages. This can be done through seminars, work groups to evolve the various parts of the change programme, task forces to work out details of implementation, etc. Participation of managers at the various stages of the change increases their commitment to the change.

Indifference of the top management: The behaviour and attitudes of the top management are critical in the implementation of change. If the top management do not show much enthusiasm or interest in the change, people at

Table 1.1: Sources of Resistance and Coping Mechanisms

Sources of Resistance	*Coping Mechanisms*
1. Perceived peripherality of change	Participation in diagnosis
2. Perception of imposition	Participation and involvement
3. Indifference of the top management	Active support from the top
4. Vested interests	Fait accompli
5. Complacency and inertia	Fait accompli
6. Fear of large scale disturbance	Phasing of change
7. Fear of inadequate resources	Support of resources
8. Fear of obsolescence	Development of skills
9. Fear of loss of power	Role redefinition and reorientation
10. Fear of overload	Role clarity and definition

Source: Introduction to Ever Changing Organisations, Gerald R. Peters and Doyle W. Young, 1999, SL Lucie Press, New York.

the lower level will have increased resistance to it. The top management can show their interest by frequently getting information and feedback in the progress of the change, participating in some seminars organized to discuss the experiences, meeting new occupants new roles created as a part of the change, providing positive strokes (encouragement and appreciation) on the success experiences, mentioning the experiment in the significant documents such as, the annual report, etc.

Vested interests: Change produces some disturbance, and sometimes some dislocation.

Complacency and inertia: As a general rule change produces discomfort. People develop complacency being in one state. The change of state is somewhat painful. The solution of the problem is to introduce the change and help people experience new conditions. Then the resistance usually goes down.

Fear of large scale disturbance: In a large organisation there may be a genuine fear that proposed is likely to lead to some changes with unpredictable consequences. This is particularly true if the proposed change is a sensitive area, and requires special skills. Phasing of the change programme may reduce resistance arising out of this dimension. Resistance to change is not always bad. Resistance plays a positive role, in indicating the areas of potential failure or problems which may come in the way of the effectiveness of the new change or system. Preventive action such as, experimentation, adjustment, phasing, etc. may be helpful.

***Fear of inadequate resources*:** Resistance may also increase if the implementation of change may require additional resources in the form of new skills, additional manpower, or budget. Provision of such resource support may reduce resistance. It may, however, be examined whether there is a genuine need for the resources. For example, if a new unit is created with greater autonomy, the support of planning, personnel and technology may be provided to help the units to succeed in meeting their objectives.

***Fear of obsolescence*:** Resistance to change may also be high if the change requires new skills and the existing people obsolete. This may be a real threat. Resistance can be partly reduced if the concerned people are given orientation and are trained in the new skills needed.

***Fear of loss of power*:** Sometimes resistance to a change is high if there is a feeling that as a result of the change some roles will lose power. Such resistance can be reduced if the roles are redefined and redesigned so that the concerned role occupants can perceive that they may have different kinds of power which may be of a higher order, although different in nature. The involved roles may be helped to realize their potential power, and develop ways of effectively using the power.

***Fear of overload*:** If some people feel that the change will increase their work load, they are likely to resist change.

This may happen if they perceive new functions being assigned to their roles. However, if their roles are defined, and they are able to prioritize the functions, and decide which functions can be delegated to their subordinates, the resistance can be reduced. This would require seminars one role definition and clarity, and negotiation for delegation of some functions. (Almaraz. J,1984)

Phases of Change

Phase I – Creativity

As illustrated in the first stage of organizational growth is called 'creativity'. In this stage the emphasis is in on creating both a product and a market. The organisation has only few employees, communication among whom is frequent and informal. The salaries of the employees are modest and they are motivated by promises of ownership benefits. But as the organisation grows and the number of its employees increases, the information communication system and the promises of ownership benefits do not work. It is at this point that the change in leadership is needed. *There is now need for a strong leader* who can pull the organisation together. Greiner calls it the "crisis of leadership".

Phase II – Direction

With the change in leadership, the next evolutionary period of growth by direction begins. The new leader in this phase follows directive techniques to harness his employees' energies into growth. He introduces a functional organisation structure, makes jobs more specialized, formalizes communication and adopts incentives and work standards. These directive techniques eventually become inappropriate for controlling a larger, more diverse and complex organisation. Lower level managers, finding themselves restricted in their functioning, resent centralized hierarchy. There is therefore, need for greater delegation. Greiner calls it the "crisis of autonomy".

Phase III – Delegation

With greater delegation, the next evolutionary period of growth begins. The organisation structure becomes decentralized. There is management by exception. But eventually, top executives start feeling that decentralization is breeding parochial attitudes. There is, therefore, need for better coordination. Greiner calls it the "crisis of control".

Phase IV-Coordination

With better and more sophisticated techniques of coordination, the next evolutionary period of growth begins. This works well for sometime and then creates another crisis- "Crisis of red tape". The whole system becomes highly bureaucratized. Staff-line conflicts become acute. There is now need for greater collaboration and team work which can be achieved by changing to a matrix type structure.

Phase V-Collaboration

With the change over to the matrix type of structure, the next evolutionary period of growth begins. During this period, economic rewards are geared to team performance. Self-discipline takes the place of a formal control system.

Strategy of Planned Change

An effective manager does not let a change occur as it will. He proactively initiates a planned change. He prepares his strategy for this purpose. Two important components of this strategy are:

(i) The dimension of change, and

(ii) The management of change.

Dimensions of Change

An organisation can usefully be viewed as a multivariate system, consisting of four interacting variables: task, structure, technology and people. Since the basic task of an organisation (e.g., manufacturing, transportation, education, social service etc.) is assumed as given, organizational change programmes can be directed towards the three remaining dimensions only, viz., structure, technology and people.(Good Enough. W., 1963)

Structural Change

Structural change aims at modifying the roles and expectations of employees by redefining man-man relationships in the organisation. This is done in three ways:

1. By replacing the key personnel. The replacement of key personnel modifies the expectations of people reporting to the new incumbents, thereby bringing about a change in man-man relationships.
2. By modifying the structure. This may be done in several ways, such as by making the organisation more centralized or decentralized, by broadening or narrowing spans of control, by redefining communication channels, by reallocating authority, by eliminating certain staff positions and so on.
3. By providing new administrative guidance. This is done by making changes in the plans, policies, budgets, procedures, methods and rules of the organisation. These result in reconstituting the role demands and expectations.

Technical Change

The technological change aims at improving the efficiency of machines and workers by changing man-job, job-job and man-man relationships. Man-job relationships are changed in two ways.

- By improving the current technology, which makes jobs easier and faster, and
- By improving the work's efficiency through time and motion, and methods studies.

Job-job relationships are changed by affecting better coordination among jobs through flow-process analysis, operation analysis, better plant lay-out and so on. Man-man relationships are changed by transferring the employee to a new group of co-employees or supervisors.

Behavioural Change

The behavioural change attempts to change the man himself by training and development. A man can be changed at three levels: knowledge, behaviour and attitude. Change in knowledge is the quickest and easiest to make. Change in behaviour is difficult. Change in attitude is most difficult. A manager's knowledge about the merits of participative decision-making may be changed quite easily by exposing him to a book or lecture. He may also be made to change his behaviour through a directive of the top head of the organisation. But it is very difficult to change his attitude towards participative decision-making, which may be the result of several influences on him of his early authoritarian upbringing.

Management of Change

One important aspect of the study of management of change is to know about the *process of change.* Kurt Lewin has identified three stages in this process. There are *unfreezing, changing* and *refreezing*. The aim of unfreezing is to motivate and make the individual or group ready to change. It is a 'thawing out' process where the force acting on an individual are so rearranged that he sees the need for rejecting old behavioural patterns and adopting new ones. In brief, unfreezing is the breaking down of the morals, customs, and traditions of an individual–the old ways of doing things–so that he is ready to accept new alternatives. According to Edgar H. Schein, the unfreezing process, to be successful, must provide for the following:

1. The physical removal of the individual, being changed from his accustomed routines, sources of information and social relationships;

2. The undermining and destruction of all social supports;
3. Demeaning and humiliating experiences to help the individual being changed to see his old self as unworthy and thus to be motivated to change; and
4. The consistent linking of reward with willingness to change and of punishment with unwillingness to change.

Once the individual has discovered the anomaly between his existing behaviour pattern and the new pattern, he enters into the metamorphosis stage. He is now ready to be provided with new patterns of behaviour. The process is most likely to occur by one of the two mechanisms: identification and internalization. *Identification* occurs when one or more models are provided in the environment from whom an individual can learn now behaviour patterns by identifying with them and trying to become like them. *Internalisation* occurs when an individual is placed in a situation where new behaviours are demands of him, if he is to operate successfully in that situation.

Refreezing is the permanent rooting of the newly acquired behaviour into the individual's personality, so that it does not get extinguished over time. If the new behaviour has been internalized while being learned, this has automatically facilitated refreezing because it has been fitted naturally into the individual's personality. If it has been learned through identification, it will persist only so long as the target's relationship with the original influence model persists. This highlights how important it is for an individual undergoing a change to be in an environment which is continually reinforcing the desired change. The effect of many a training programme has been short-lived when the person returns to an environment that does not reinforce the new pattern or even worse, is hostile toward it.

The most important thing in refreezing is that the new behaviour does not get extinguished over time. To ensure that this doest not happen reinforcement (reward and incentives) must be scheduled in an effective way. There seem to be two main reinforcement schedules–continuous and intermittent. Continuous reinforcement means that the individual beings changed is rewarded *every time* he engages in the desired new pattern. With intermittent reinforcement, on the other hand, not every desired response is reinforced. With continuous reinforcement the individual learns the new behaviour quickly, but if his environment changes to one of non-reinforcement, extinction (elimination of the behaviour) can be expected to take place relatively soon. With intermittent reinforcement, extinction is much slower because the individual has been conditioned to go for periods of time without any reinforcement. Thus for fast learning, a continuous reinforcement schedule should be used. But one the individual has learned the new pattern, a switch to intermittent reinforcement should ensure a long lasting change.

Resistance to Change

Out of the three stages of the process of change, the unfreezing stage is perhaps the most difficult because it is in this stage that a manager has to face maximum resistance from his employees. The reasons for this resistance are as follows:

1. People resist changes which are against their habits, experiences, perceptions, customs, beliefs and values.
2. People resist change which they think will alter their established human relationships in the organisation. This is the social aspect of a change. It is now well established on the basis of experience and research that people show greater resistance to change in the social aspect than to change in the technical aspect. This is due to the following two reasons:

   (a) Benefits of change in the social aspect of a job cannot be so convincingly measured and demonstrated as benefits of change in its technical aspect.

(b) People's attachment to the social aspects of a job is generally based on emotions, which they cannot easily overcome but their attachment to the technical aspect of a job is always based on some purpose. Hence people easily give up an inferior technology in the face of superior technology which claims to serve their purpose better.

3. People also resist change because of it following repercussions;

   (a) It may destroy the public image of their job.

   (b) It may lower the ranking of their job vis-à-vis other jobs.

   (c) It may render their existing skills obsolete and may make retraining necessary.

   (d) It may increase discipline in the workplace.

   (e) It may impose higher performance standards on them.

   (f) It may throw them out of employment or reduce their promotion prospects.

Introducting Change: Directive and Participative Methods

Broadly speaking, there are two methods of introducing a planned change: directive method and participative method. In directive method, the employer unilaterally decrees that certain changes will take place. In participative method, the employer lets his employees come up with the proposed changes. In between these 2 methods there can be several other variations allowing employees different degrees of latitude, both in problem identification, as well as in problem solving.

Choice between Directive and Participative Methods

It is useful to remember the following points while making a choice between directive and participative methods.

Employees' maturity level. Directive method is more appropriate when the employees are immature or when they are not willing to accept the change unless forced to do so or when the situation is chaotic. The participative method is more appropriate when the employees are quite mature, achievement-motivated and willing to accept the change.

Position power of the change agent. The directive method is more appropriate when the agent of change enjoys sufficient position power, e.g., he has significant control over reward and punishments. But if he enjoys only reference or expert power, participative methods would be more appropriate.

Communication pattern in the organisation. Directive method is more appropriate if the organisation's communication pattern is of the star-type, which favours the change-agent as a leader over his subordinates. But if the pattern is of the circle type, the change-agent will face some difficulty if he attempts to introduce change in a directive manner.

Balance of forces. Devised by Kurt Lewin, the Force Field Analysis is a helpful tool to compare the number and strength of forces as the driving forces and the restraining forces, respectively. The directive method can be successful only when the driving forces far outweigh the restraining forces. In the opposite situation, when the restraining forces are stronger than the driving forces, introduction of change by directive method will give a further fillip to the restraining forces and is, therefore, not advisable. The participative methods is successful, both when the forces welcoming the change are stronger and when they are weaker than the forces opposing the change.

Consequences. Directive method introduces the change in behaviour immediately but it creates resentment and hostility. The change introduced by this method is very often short-lived. It lasts only as long as the maintenance efforts continue or the driving forces outweigh the restraining forces. As soon as the maintenance efforts cease or the driving forces reduce, back sliding takes place because people in the organisation have not participated enough to internalize the change. It may be noted that this is the typical experience of all managements by drives e.g., cost-reduction drive, safety drive etc. By participative method, the change in behaviour is introduced slowly (via change in attitudes) but it develops involvement and commitment. The change is permanent and lasting. It does not need any efforts to maintain itself.

Organizational Orientation to Change

When organisations are examined closely for the behaviours, systems, and structures that impact their capacity for change, they fall somewhere on the continuum in terms of their overall orientation to change. These features of the organisation's design reflect the assumptions of those who created them. They send clear messages to the members of the organisation and its stakeholders about the change orientation and expectations of management. It is consistent with their perceptions of what is expected and valued. As a result, the organisation's position on the orientation to change continuum has direct influence on the ability of the organisation to anticipate, cope with, or manage the demands for change with which it is faced. And failure to meet those demands is a prescription for eventual failure. The process of organisations Change Management can be seen in Figure 1.5.

To reach a conclusion about where an organisation falls on the continuum many questions must be asked. The organisation's policies and procedures must be reviewed their underlying values and assumptions identified. Business process and the constraints under which they operate are explored. Executives, managers, and other members of the organisation are interviewed and observed to understand their behaviours and the underlying assumptions and values they act upon in relating to change.

Fig. 1.5.

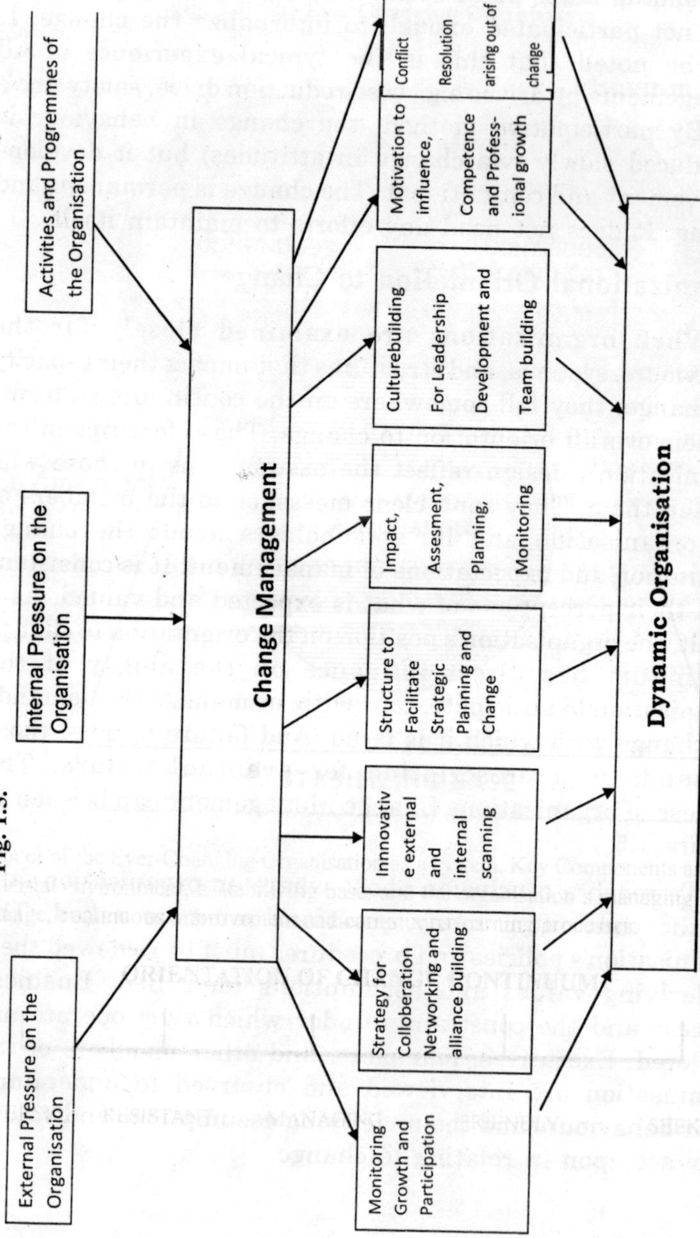

Source : Gareth Morgan, *Creative Organisation Theory- A resource book*, Sage Publications 1989.

1. Change Averse

On the far left of the continuum organisations whose orientation is "change averse." Change is something to be avoided and prevented. Change is perceived as disruptive – as something that takes people's focus from their real jobs. Energy is devoted to keeping things the way they are. Management is reluctant to initiate changes. Continuous improvement and learning processes are not developed. People are not involved or empowered to make changes and improvements. Top down, institutional control predominates with decisions reserved for the highest levels only. Customers, with the changes they are perceived to force on the organisation, are considered a necessary evil and competitors are the enemy.

2. Change Resistant

"Change-resistant" organisations have long lists of reasons why changes are a bad idea and will fail. They prefer stability and performance and want to avoid the messiness associated with change. Decisions to change are delayed, sometimes until there is no choice. People are expected to do what they have been asked or told to do and not to look for and propose changes. Their jobs are seen, at this point on the continuum, as simply "doing." Issues with customers, suppliers, or other external agencies are responded to when the demands are great enough to get attention at the highest levels. Learning is left to the individual. When change does occur it is inevitably at the initiation of top management or in response to some externally imposed requirement that cannot be argued away. Top down control of decisions and complex, multilevel approvals are required for change and other actions, even those that have been previously accepted.

3. Change Managing

At the midpoint of the continuum, organisations acknowledge the CSOs in nature of change. Stability and permanence are preferred, but these organisations accept change as part of their world and are prepared to adapt to the forces for change. When the forces for change are seen as necessary or imposed by external requirements where resistance is not useful or could be counterproductive, the organisation works to manage the change process. Not much is done to anticipate required change, but when faced with the need these organisations do what is necessary. They recognize that the process of change can be managed to make it more successful as well as less disruptive and time consuming. The greater effectiveness of planned change is viewed as worth the investment. Some level of decision making and spending authority regarding change is given to middle levels of the organisation but probably not below. People are informed about change decisions and sometimes participate in the process of planning the changes. Opportunities for involvement in continuous improvement and continuous learning become part of the organisation's process. People are trained in the needed skills for learning and improvement. Customers are viewed as critical to the organisation's success and processes are designed to stay in touch with customers and their needs. The organisation shares its needs and plants with its suppliers.

4. *Change Friendly*

From this point on the continuum, and to the right, organisations implement or redesign systems and processes to make change easier. Barriers to change and improvement are identified and removed. People throughout the organisation are provided skills, tools, and time for participation in continuous learning and improvement activities. Mapping of key business processes becomes a major tool for facilitating change. People are empowered in their individual jobs and in their work units to identify and eliminate the sources of defects and to find ways to improve work processes, e.g., reduce cycle times, eliminate non-value-added activities, reduce waste and rework, and so on.

5. Change Seeking

"Change seeking" organisations value change and fear failure to change. They believe that "to stand still is to regress and their beginning of dying." Continuous improvement and continuous learning are more than phrases, they are values that are integrated into the organisation. Lifelong learning at the individual and organizational levels is espoused and supported by the organisation's policies and systems as well as by its financial backing. Extensive processes are designed for sensing and anticipating the external world in all respects. Customer communication and focus is an obsession. Competitive intelligence is pursued aggressively. Technological changes are examined constantly for opportunities to create new products and services. Potential actions of external agencies are monitored vigorously. These actions are for the purpose of creating change – leading and not being forced to follow. Change seekers define the competitive agenda. They strive to satisfy customers' needs before others are able to. People are viewed as the organisation's most critical assets. This belief is reflected in the way they are developed and how their capabilities are used. Clear statements of the organisation's vision and values and an understanding of their implications guide each person's behaviour. Self-management and control is understood to be much more powerful than external control, and well-skilled and informed people are assumed to be able to make appropriate choices for changes for themselves and the organisation.

6. Implications of Orientation to Change

The intent of the orientation to change continuum is to be descriptive, not evaluative. Where an organisation falls on the continuum is neither inherently good nor bad. Where issues arise for an organisation derives from whether the orientation to change is functional or dysfunctional, i.e., whether or not the orientation towards change helps the organisation in the context of its business and environment.

In more stable environments there will generally be less need for a strong change orientation. And, to the extent that the management of the organisation has made reasoned choices in this are, being more resistant or less change friendly can serve the organisation positively. Yet, even historically more stable environments have become less stable and demanding of greater receptivity to change, both internally and externally.

Also the changes in technology and the opportunities presented. Failure to acquire and use the technology may not be fatal in the short run, but long delays are likely to put businesses at a competitive disadvantage.

Managing for Change

Impetus for change

The key questions in the area of impetus of change have to do with what triggers change activity in the organisation and where in the organisation changes originate. The impetus for change in situations where managing for change is strong, comes from any and all parts of the organisation.

1. Change as Everyone's Responsibility

Change-averse or change-resistant organisations highly restrict the responsibility for initiating change. Organisations that are managed FOR change, on the other hand, broaden the range of responsibility for change. With high impetus for change, identifying and initiating change is explicitly defined as part of each person's responsibility. Waiting to be asked is inappropriate. Each person is assumed to be aware of needs for change and the issues that impact the performance of their work. Living with the job on a day-to-day basis produces insights that are unavailable to anyone else.

Yet the initiation of ideas for change is not left to chance. Time is made available for examining one's work performance and exploring ways to improve. This might be done by individuals but is more likely to be done in groups. Members of work teams meet regularly, and one of the continuing agenda items is consideration of ways to improve their work processes and performance. Participation in benchmarking studies or, at a minimum being informed of benchmarking results, is another sources of ideas about what's possible and ways to change to make the new possibilities happen.

People in organisations high in managing FOR change also are provided measurements and data about the performance of their unit. They are given the opportunity to visit with people on their areas, i.e., their internal customers or suppliers, to understand how their performance impacts, or is impacted by others. Exchange visits are arranged with people in similar jobs in other companies to broaden awareness of the work processes or equipment employed and how they might relate to potential changes in their own work. The result of data provided to people and the outcome of these visits is an increased capacity of those involved to manage their own work for change. They do not have to rely on others for ideas and are able to translate their observations and discussions directly into making change and improvements in their own areas.(Drucker, Peter F., 1996)

2. Problems or Opportunities?

Organisations with high impetus for change are looking for ways to improve no matter what the reason. If problems exist, the focus is on resolving them. But the emphasis is not on simply stopping the problem. Instead, focus is on understanding the cause of the problem and corrective action that keeps it from happening again. Knowing the root cause of a problem leads to solutions aimed at preventing recurrence as opposed to changes that fix the immediate problem but not the underlying cause.

People throughout organisations with high impetus for change understand the importance of seeking opportunities for change in addition to solving problems. Management's behaviour clearly communicates its support of people's efforts to improve, with particular attention to being proactive. Prevention of problems frees up time previously consumed in reactive problem resolution. People learn tools for mapping work processes and use those maps to explore opportunities for change and improvement.

3. Incremental or Breakthrough Change?

We have been surprised by the number of arguments that arise regarding the importance of incremental changes vs breakthrough change. Some argue that the principal of "kaizen" common in Japanese improvement efforts is slow and even has the potential to stifle creativity when everyone is looking for ways to make a 1% improvement in several hundred areas. Others argue that looking for breakthrough opportunities and only supporting major change efforts cuts off gains possible from a significant percentage of the resources available to the organisation.

4. Change Stemming from the Absence of Change

Where impetus for change is high, questions are raised when specified periods of time have passed without any change. This behavior is based on the assumption that improvement is always possible. The failure to identify and initiate changes within a period of a few to several months triggers questions about the improvement process, not the assumption that the work process needs no improvement. Obstacles to change are identified and, as necessary, removed to get the improvement process moving gain.

Many organisations recognize that established policies or rules often do not change, despite other changes that render them impractical or obsolete. Those with a high impetus for change go beyond being aware of this condition to acting on it. Periodic reviews and updates of policy manuals and operating procedures are required to assure that existing ones are updated and changed when they are no longer relevant. The concept of "sunset causes" is attractive to these organisations. Instead of providing for continuation of policies or rules, they are required to include a time for termination. Unless the policy or rule is reconfirmed to be of value — by the issuer as well as by those affected — it must be rewritten to make it relevant and useful or it dies. With high impetus for change, organisations are unwilling to tolerate continuation of irrelevant and obsolete practices. Instead of allowing them to continue, the absence of change causes the "sun to set" and they are eliminated.

Change Planning Management

An organisation working to increase its capacity has to create effective processes for the planning and management of any change effort. The organisation cannot be said to be managing for change without such processes. Change-averse or resistant organisations generally have not established methods for dealing with change. It is dealt with primarily by brute force. Changes are announced and implemented and people are expected comply with whatever is handed to them. They are not given the opportunities to participate in either the decision to change or in planning the implementation of change that impacts their work.

1. Predictable Responses to Imposed Change

A number of people have written about the effects of imposed change. They describe a predictable series of emotional responses in people. These reactions are normal and are neither anti organizational responses to be suppressed nor indications of a natural resistance to change.

The typical initial response to imposed change is some form of denial that the change will happen. Evidence of the certainty of the change is needed to move people beyond the period of denial. With continuation of the change effort, however, a phase of resistance appears. Responses range from ignoring the change to explaining why it won't work or will only make things worse to actually sabotaging efforts to implement to change. People eventually move beyond resistance if, or when, they have had the opportunity to work through the issues influencing their resistance. They then move into a phase where they examine the positive sides of the change, exploring how it will benefit them and how they will use it. Once this has been accomplished, there is movement into the last phase. At that point belief in the change and a personal commitment to make it work develops.

Organisations where change planning and management is lacking either do not understand that these phases of response to change occur or believe that they can use their power and influence to force people into being committed to a change. Changes are often introduced with lots of hype and hoopla. People are told what will happen and when and that the change is important for the success of the organisation. They are asked to signify their acceptance and buy-in to the change in some way such as signing a pledge or becoming part of a team to make the change happen.

Management and change leaders (often the same people) leave these sessions with a sense that the change has been sold and people are committed to make it happen. They have done nothing to help their people deal with their feelings of resistance or their need to understand "What is in it for me". And they will not understand the resistance that appears later and the accompanying delays in implementing the change.

Executives and change leaders in organisations have created conditions that produce the illusion of commitment via symbolic acts that people feel compelled to take. They still need to work through feelings of resistance, to become comfortable that the outcomes of the change are not threatening, and to explore how the change affects them before they reach a real state of commitment.

2. *Change Planning and Management Factors*

Organisations strong in change-planning and management are aware that people must go through the various phases of responding to the change. They legitimize their reasons the support people through the phases of change. They realize that people cannot simply jump from hearing about a change to fully accepting and committing to it. Some time will be required, and management provides for that in their planning. Following are some ideas for improving the effectiveness of change-planning and management.

a) Use Understanding of the Phases of Change

Explain the organisation's awareness that there will be reactions to the change, including feelings of resistance and concerns about how it affects each person. Acknowledge that these reactions are normal and appropriate and that time will be provided to discuss people's concerns. Then provide them with an opportunity to explore the implications of the change for themselves. Make this exploration two-way and with their supervisors and managers (this should be taken to apply to middle-and upper-level executives as well as to those at the lowest levels of the organisation). Should I be concerned that the changes will negatively impact me personally? Will I have to learn new skills or ways of working or will the change fit into how we operate now? How can we know that getting excited about the change and putting our effort into making it succeed will be worth it vs. having this be another new thing that starts and then dies? And so on. Legitimizing and dealing with these issues helps people move more rapidly through the phases of denial and resistance and on to examination of the change for its benefits and uses. The investment of time in planning and supporting such processes is well worth the effort and is characteristic of organisations high on change planning and management.

b) Minimize Imposed Change and Maximize Participation

Research has demonstrated that participation in decisions to change and/or in planning for the implementation of change has strikingly positive influence on the outcomes of the change.

What is needed in situations of greater participation is for management to provide the boundaries within which the participation will occur. The manager may clearly reserve certain decisions for him/herself. Even with those decisions, however, it may be that there would be participation in plans for how to implement the decisions. With the boundaries clarified, managers can work with their people to build a set of criteria and ground rules for involvement and how they will work. An important example would be the need to establish who gets involved and how decisions are made when time is not available for the entire group to work on the issue. Or, which decisions will involve the group and which will engage subgroups or individuals? Establishing common and shared expectations makes it much easier to manage the participative process.

c) Capitalize On the Energy Released by Change

Energy is released when change occurs. That energy can end up being used in ways that support the change or make implementation more difficult. Where change-planning and management are weak the energy is often exhibited as obstruction and resistance. Consider, for example, the amount of time and energy spent in hallway discussions or behind closed doors when changes are announced or imminent. The expenditure of energy is very high, non-productive, and primarily speculative.

On the other hand, actively involving people in developing plans for implementing a change and making it work positively focuses the energy to the advantage of the people and the organisation. Concerns and sources of resistance are addressed in the process and buy-in is developed for the change more easily. Those involved feel ownership of the implementation plan and personally committed to its success.

d) Assess and Develop Readiness for Change

Highly capable organisations in the areas of change planning and management invest the effort needed to assess readiness for change. They create plans to improve readiness and to reduce or eliminate conditions that will contribute to failure. They recognize that the effort involved is minimal compared to that which will be required to recover from a poorly planned and managed change process.

Many questions are asked and the answers used to optimize the probability of success. Is there a leader for the change whose skills are appropriate for the task and whose leadership will be accepted? Are those support it critical to success on board or are likely to be obstacles? If so, what is needed to gain their support or, at a minimum, to prevent them from behaving in ways that could cause the change to fail? What resources and support are needed (time, people, and financial) and have they been allocated? How will the success of the effort be measured? Is there a communication plan in place for the introduction of the change and for keeping people informed of progress? Can the reasons for the change be articulated and supported with logic and fact? Will the people of the organisation understand why the change is occurring and what's in it for them? Has an analysis been done of potentially serious problems and plans developed to prevent their occurrence or to minimize their effect? And so on.

Some organisations never ask these questions or ignore the date if they become available. They are so action-oriented that processes for developing readiness seem wasteful. Yet they often end up spending even more time after the change is introduced dealing with resistance and other actions required to "sell" the change. Such groups are clearly lacking in change-planning and management and fall at the change-averse or, minimally, change-resistant point of our change orientation scale.

2

Evolution of Civil Society Organisations

Though the term has existed since early times, civil society as an intellectual construct gained clarity and lucidity with the advent of modernity in the western world during the 17th century. Many events like the growth of the institutions of private property, spread of urbanization, contributed immensely to the meaning of the term 'civil society'. However, it is the rise of capitalism that led to a clear distinction between political and non-political and thus prepared the ground for the emergence of civil society as a separate domain, to be seen independent from, yet via-a-vis the state, as an intermediary layer between individuals and families, on the one hand, and state institutions on the other.

Since then the concept 'civil society' has been bestowed with many meanings and has undergone many revisions. Some theories of civil society position it as a 'space' independent of the state and the market; other equate it with the voluntary sector. For Seligman, civil society is an ethical ideal which holds the public and the private in a balance; for Tandon, civil society initiatives represent those achieving common public good. For Tocqueville and Putnam, civil society is a network of associations and applications which safeguard democratic space between the state and the family.

The contemporary interest in civil society has arisen out of the collapse of the communist regime in East-Central Europe. Resurrection of this concept and its use in the past decade was necessitated, as significant shifts in the roles of the state and the market began to be articulated.

In the contemporary interpretations of civil society, therefore, three distinctive approaches can be noted. The first approach is essentially derived from the Anglo-American tradition and builds on the work of Tocqueville, and more recently of Putnam who saw solidarity among people expressed through associations, helps in curbing the authoritarian tendencies of the state and promoting democratic culture. The representative form of democracy creates a distance between state institutions and their decision-making from individuals and families who are relatively powerless. Building solidarity and associations across citizens helps them to mediate and negotiate their aspirations and interests with the state.

The second meaning of civil society has arisen from the challenge posed by people to communist regimes in Eastern Europe and military dictatorship in Latin America, Philippines, and South Africa. The thrust of these people's movements was to democratize the state and create fundamental freedom and liberties for their citizens. In such a formulation, civil society began to be equated with the process of democratization in political structures and systems.

A third approach to the notion of civil society has its roots in the rise of neo-liberalism and spread of free market and private enterprise all over the world. Public Sector (the state and its institutions) and Private Sector (the for-profit business enterprise) have been undergoing realignments and shifts in their roles and relative contributions to societal development. In this formulation "Third Sector" formations (which include community based organisations, voluntary organisations, philanthropic endeavours, religious associations etc.) now being re-conceptualised as civil society, are seen as having the potential to augment social development.

Defining Civil Society

Civil society inhabits the area between individuals (or families) and the state, and is made up of associational groupings of all sorts. In its widest sense, civil society would range from political parties on the more public side of this terrain over to business corporations on the more private side and it would include groups aiming to influence the formation and implementation of public policy as well as groups that have no concern for the public domain at all.

In constructing an operationalisable approach to civil society, however it makes sense to narrow the definition so that it embraces primarily non-governmental organisations (CSOs) emphasizing public rather than private goals, or more specifically, voluntary groups concerned *inter alea* with influencing state policy. A concentration on influencing the state need not be an CSO's principal concern for it to be of interest here, but such a focus must bé an least a significant part of the group's activities. Thus we would exclude such essentially single-purpose organisations as a business enterprise or a political party; the former's main goal is to make a profit, while the latter's is to take over state power (as opposed to influencing it, as with the institutions of civil society).

The characteristic institution of civil society to what we may call a 'civil society organisation' (CSO), which can be defined as CSO, that has as one of its primary purposes influencing public policy. Thus while all NGOs are CSOs, by no means all CSOs are also NGOs. In most Third World systems, only a portion of the total society is included within the total universe of CSOs, and only a portion of the NGOs are also CSOs. A purely service-oriented CSO (say, in the health by the same token a CSO could become an NGO if it dropped its advocacy activities to concentrate solely on service delivery.

One useful way to think of civil society is to characterize it as having a kind of 'in-betweenness'. In its usual definition, civil society lies between the state on one side and the individual or family on the other,. But civil society also sits between what is usually thought of as the public and private sectors (some writers see it as a 'third sector' in addition to these two). And there is an additional dimension as well, in that CSOs are usually not (although some may be) profit-seeking, but neither are they generally what we think of as non-profit, service-providing organisations (though at times they might be). To sum up, civil society comprises the collectivity of those social organisations that enjoy *autonomy from the state* (are not a part of the state or creatures of it) and have as one important goal among others to *influence the state* on behalf of their members.(Gann, N. 1986)

Civil Society and Democratic Development

1. The idea of 'civil society' has a long history, tracing back to Hobbes and Hegel, but in its contemporary usage it has come into the political science literature only quite recently; earlier terms with a similar meaning were 'interest groups' or 'pressure groups', but these were applied largely to the political systems of the advanced industrial countries. Today 'civil society' is the term most widely used to describe this sector in the development field.

2. The 'state' as used here has been in widespread usage at least since the mid-1980s – longer than 'civil society' but still relatively new in its meaning here as the whole set of governmental organisations, ranging from local to national, that make and enforce rules for the society. The state is thus not only the political leadership or the bureaucracy, and it does not exist only at the national or (as in the United States) intermediate level, but rather it is the collectivity of office-holding political leaders and bureaucracy at all levels.

3. Some political parties may be included in civil society by this definition, if their primary goal is to act as a pressure group rather than take power, some of the European Green parties would be examples here. The number of such parties in the Third World is probably small, however, especially in the absence of the proportional representation

electoral systems that tend to encourage their continuance in the western European political scene.

What Civil Society Can Do?

By civil society, it means the entire range of organized groups and institutions that are dependent of the state, voluntary, and at least to some extent self-generating and self-reliant. This of course includes non-governmental organizations but also independent mass media, think tanks, universities, and social and religious groups.

To be part of civil society, groups must meet some other conditions as well. In a democracy, civil society groups have respect for the law, for the rights of individuals, and for the rights of other groups to express their interests and opinions. Part of what the word "civil" implies is tolerance and the accommodation of pluralism and diversity.

Civil society groups may establish ties to political parties and the state, but they must retain their independence, and they do not seek political power for themselves.

Often in transitions, groups arise that seek to monopolize the lives and thinking of their members. These groups do not tolerate the right of their members to dissent, and they do not respect other groups that disagree with them. Some of these groups may merely be fronts for political parties or movements that seek to win control of the state. These groups are not part of civil society.

What, then, can the independent, voluntary, law-abiding, tolerant and pluralistic organisations of civil society do?

The first and most basic role of civil society is to limit and control the power of the state.

Civil society actors should watch how state officials use their powers. They should raise public concern about any abuse of power. They should lobby for access to information, including freedom of information laws, and rules and institutions to control corruption.

This constitutes a second important function of civil society: to expose the corrupt conduct of public officials and lobby for good governance reforms. Even where anti-corruption laws and bodies exist, they cannot function effectively without the active support and participation of civil society.

A third function of civil society is to promote political participation. CSOs can do this by educating people about their rights and obligations as democratic citizens and encouraging them to listen to election campaigns and vote in elections. CSOs can also help develop citizens' skills to work with one another to solve common problems, to debate public issues, and express their views.

Fourth, civil society organizations can help to develop the other values of democratic life: tolerance, moderation, compromise, and respect for opposing points of view.

Fifth, civil society also can help to develop programs for democratic civic education in the schools as well. After dictatorship, comprehensive reforms are needed to revise the curricula, rewrite the textbooks, and retrain teachers in order to educate young people about the crimes of the past and teach them the principles and values of democracy. Civil society must be involved as a constructive partner and advocate for democracy and human rights training.

Sixth, civil society is an arena for the expression of diverse interests, and one role for civil society organizations is to lobby for the needs and concerns of their members, as women, students, farmers, environmentalists, trade unionists, lawyers, doctors, and so on CSOs and interest groups can present their views to parliament and provincial councils, by contacting individual members and testifying before parliamentary committees. They can also establish a dialogue with relevant government ministries and agencies to lobby for their interests and concerns.

A seventh duty of civil society is to provide new forms of interest and solidarity that cut across old forms of tribal, linguistic religious and other identity ties. When people of different religions and ethnic identities come together on the basis of their common interests as women, artists, doctors, students, workers, farmers, lawyers, human rights activists, environmentalists, and so on, civic life becomes richer, more complex, and more tolerant.

Eighth, civil society can provide a training ground for future political leaders. CSOs and other groups can help to identify and train new types of leaders who have dealt with important public issues. Experience from other countries shows that civil society is a particularly important arena from which to recruit and train future women leaders.

Ninth, civil society can help to inform the public about important public issues. This is not only the role of the mass media, but of CSOs which can provide forums for debating public policies and disseminating information about issues before parliament that affect the interests of different groups, or of society at large.

Tenth, civil society organizations can play an important role in mediating and helping to resolve conflict. In other countries, CSOs have developed formal programs and training of trainers to relieve political and ethnic conflict and teach groups to solve their disputes through bargaining and accommodation.

Eleventh, civil society organizations have a vital role to play in monitoring the conduct of elections. This requires a broad coalition of organizations, unconnected to political parties or candidates.

CSOs Types by Orientation

(Source:Course material for Post Graduation Diploma in Rural Management(RDD-3), The Indira Gandhi National Open University School of Continuing Education, New Delhi)

Charitable Orientation often involves a top-down paternalistic effort with little participation by the "beneficiaries". It includes CSOs with activities directed toward meeting the needs of the poor -distribution of food, clothing or medicine; provision of housing, transport, schools etc. Such CSOs may also undertake relief activities during a natural or man- made disaster,

Service Orientation includes CSOs with activities such as the provision of health, family planning or education services in which the programme is designed by the CSOs and people are expected to participate in its implementation and in receiving the service.

Participatory Orientation is characterized by self-help projects where local people are involved particularly in the implementation of a project by contributing cash, tools, land, materials, labour etc. In the classical community development project, participation begins with the need definition and continues into the planning and implementation stages. Cooperatives often have a participatory orientation.

Empowering Orientation is where the aim is to help poor people develop a clearer understanding of the social, political and economic factors affecting their lives, and to strengthen their awareness of their own potential power to control their lives. Sometimes, these groups develop spontaneously around a problem or an issue, at other times outside workers from CSOs play a facilitating role in their development. In any case, there is maximum involvement of the people with CSOs acting as facilitators.

CSO Types by Level Operation

Community based organisations (CBOs) arise out of people's own initiatives. These can include sports clubs, Women's Organisations, Neighbourhood Organisations, Religious or Educational organisations..

There are a large variety of these, some supported by CSOs, national or international CSOs, or bilateral or international agencies, and others independent of outside help. Some are devoted to rising the consciousness of the urban poor or helping them to understand their rights in gaining access to needed services while others are involved in providing such services.

Citywide Organisations include organisations such as the rotary or Lion's Club, Chambers of Commerce and Industry, Coaliations of Business, Ethnic or Educational groups and Associations of Community Organisations. Some exist for other purposes, and become involved in helping the poor as one of many activities, while others are created for the specific purpose of helping the poor.

National CSOs include organisations such as the Red Cross, YMCAs/YWCAs, Professional Organisations etc. Some of the se have state and country branches and assist local CSOs.

International CSOs range from secular gencies such as Agakhan Foundation and Save the Children organizations, OXFAM, CARE, Ford and Rockefeller Foundations to religiously motivated groups. Their activities vary from mainly funding local CSOs, institutions and projects, to implementing the projects themselves (Table 2.1)

World Bank and Other Definitions of a CSO

(Source: Course material for Post Graduation Diploma In Rural Management(RDD-4), The Indira Gandhi National Open University School of Continuing Education, New Delhi).

"The diversity of CSO strains any simple definition. They include many groups and institutions that are entirely or largely independent of government and that have primarily humanitarian or cooperative rather than commercial objectives. They are private agencies in industrial countries that support

international development; indigenous groups organized regionally or nationally; and member-groups in villages. CSOs include charitable and religious associations that mobilize private funds for development, distribute food and family planning services and promote community organization. They also include independent cooperatives, community associations, water-user societies, women's groups and pastoral associations. Citizen Groups that raise awareness and influence policy are also CSO".

Various Definitions of CSO

CSO

A non-profit making, voluntary, service-oriented/ development oriented organization, either for the benefit of members (a grassroots organization) or of other members of the population (an agency).

CSO

It is an organization of private individuals who believe in certain basic social principles and who structure their activities to bring about development to communities that they are servicing.

CSO

Social Development Organization assisting in empowerment of people.

CSO

An organization or group of people working independent of any external control with specific objectives and aims to fulfil tasks that are oriented to bring about desirable change in a given community or area or situation.

CSO

An independent, democratic, non-sectarian peoples organization working for the empowerment of economic and/ or socially marginalized groups.

Table 2.1: Three Generations of CSOs Development Programme Strategies

	First	*Second*	*Third*
Defining Features	Relief and Welfare	Small-scale, self-reliant local development	Sustainable systems development
Problem Definition	Shortages of goods and services	Local inertia	Institutional and policy constraints
Time Frame	Immediate	Project life	Indefinite long-term
Spatial Scope	Individual or family	Neighbourhood or village	Region or nation
Chief Actors	CSO	CSO + beneficiary organisations	All public and private institutions that define the relevant system
Development Education	Starving children	Community self-help initiatives	Failures in interdependent systems
Management Orientation	Logistics management	Project management	Strategic management

Source : Korten, David, "Third Generation CSO Strategies: A Key to People-centered Development". Paper presented at the CSO Workshop organized at the Asian Institute of Technology, Bangkok, October 17-21, 1988.

CSO

An organization not affiliated to political parties, generally engaged in working for aid, development and welfare of the community.

CSO

Organization committed to the root causes of the problems trying to better the quality of life especially for the poor, the oppressed, the marginalized in urban and rural areas.

CSO

Organizations established by and for the community without or with little intervention from the government; they are not only a charity organization, but work on socio-economic-cultural activities.

CSO

An organization that is flexible and democratic in its organization and attempts to serve the people without profit for itself.

At its simplest, *civil society is the arena in which people come together to pursue the interests they hold in common* - not for profit or political power, but because they care enough about something to take collective action. It is:

- "the space of un-coerced human action"
- "the vehicle through which people take action as moral beings"
- "all organisations and associations above the level of the family and below the level of the state".

Where did Civil Society Come From?

Western theories see it as the product of the nation state and industrial capitalism; the Liberals claim it arose spontaneously to mediate conflicts between social life and the market economy when the industrial revolution fractured traditional bonds of kin and community; Marxists argue that it was deliberately organised by those who suffered under capitalism as a counterweight to exploitation. Non-Western theories, on the other hand, see civil society at work in all countries and stages of development, but expressed in different ways according to history and context. Since nation states are largely a creation of colonialism and the market economy often has only a fragile hold, civil societies in the South are bound to differ from those in the North. As globalisation proceeds, the geography of markets changes and state sovereignty is eroded; that has implications for civil societies too, which the Liberal approach largely ignores.

What Does It Look Like?

Western theories visualize civil society as one of three circles (along with the state and the market), separate from and independent of each-other, though they may overlap in the middle. Each sector has a clear role and competence which doesn't change over time, or from one society to another: markets produce, states govern, and civil societies do the things that the other two sectors cannot or will not do. "If states and markets worked perfectly", as an American professor put it, civil society would disappear." Non-Western theories emphasis that the borders between sectors are always "fuzzy." Real life is characterized by connections and overlaps between institutions; roles and responsibilities continually evolve; and hybrid institutions emerge from the resulting mixture (like the Grameen Bank - part CSO, part business). State, civil society and market continually interact with each-other, and that is what produces change. Civil societies contribute something additional; they are not just a consequence of state and market failure.

Does Civil Society Really make a Difference?

It is impossible to make sense of the civil society debate in isolation from the ends to which civil society is supposed to be a means. Yet the transmission mechanisms between a "strong civil society" and development goals are not well-understood. At the level of national development performance, experience shows that the synergy between a strong state and a strong society is one of the keys to sustained, poverty-reducing growth. This does not mean a strong civil society Western-style, but it does mean a dense network of intermediary associations that act as a counterweight to vested interests, promote institutional accountability among states and markets, channel information to decision-makers on what is happening at the "sharp end", and negotiate the "contracts" between government and citizens that development requires

-I'll scratch your back by delivering growth, investment and services; you scratch mine by delivering wage restraint or absorbing the costs of welfare.

Civil Society Organisations. Some Insights

CSOs – Identity beyond Definition

Voluntary Associations – Part Of Social Order

For centuries, human societies were being regulated by social orders and structures. These structures acquired credibility and acceptance in managing the complex human life and in maintaining the rhythm of civilized life.

Commonly accepted basic social orders are Society, State, Market and Associations. Human life is sought to be nurtured by these orders, namely, households, governmental agencies, private enterprises, voluntary associations and non-governmental organisations. In terms of sectoral paradigm the following tiers could be broadly identified.

First Sector : Public (government)

Second Sector: Private business (profit oriented)

Third Sector : Voluntary associations / Voluntary organisations and civil society organisation (people's participation without profit motive)

Coexistence and complementality of these social orders is necessary to promote all round, balanced and integrated development of all citizens and country as a whole.

Emergence of CSOs on Stage of Development

It is pertinent to recall that India has a great tradition of social service, social reforms and voluntary community based service from time immemorial.

Ever since pre-independence era, voluntary associations and organisations in India have been playing a crucial constructive role in society building. Initially associated with the tasks of social service, social reforms and nationalism, voluntary organisations plunged into independence movement. Thereafter these have expanded eventually in the post-independence éra and entered into new horizons of development. Many of these organisations continued to follow Gandhian philosophy and have been assisting in the activities of national building in areas of health, literacy and emancipation of the under- privileged sections. As social work acquired new insights and perspectives with the interventions of State from panchayat level, the bases of these organisations have also undergone several structural changes. While a few voluntary organisations have chosen to confine themselves to chosen tasks, new organisations have entered the development process availing support of government in the form of grants and legal entitlements. They have chartered their activities in tandem with governmental programmes.

While some voluntary organisations chose philanthropic and relief activities, new organisations that have emerged sought financial assistance of State to gear up their activities along with planned development programmes launched by government. Thus Civil Society Organisations (CSOs) have made their presence felt on the centre stage of development.

The second stage of growth of CSOs in India came about the '60s. A large number of organisations championing the cause of poor, landless, tribals, the bonded labour/child labour, women, etc. have emerged on the scene. These organisations were small, scattered and operated at village level.

Third stage of growth of CSOs came about much later with the commitment of Central Government in the VI Five Plan Document (1980-85) identifying specific areas of development for partnership with CSOs. The Seventh Plan (1985-90) envisaged a more proactive role for CSOs so as to make communities as self-reliant as possible.

In the past two decades, there has been astronomical increase in the number of CSOs due to increasing awareness and social concern for the widespread poverty and deprivation.

Today India has a vibrant CSO sector. Although the actual number of such organisations is not available through complete census, total number is, however, estimated to be over 1,00,000 of which 30% are active.

UNO Definition of CSO – Unrealistic in Indian Context

The word CSO was mainly coined by United Nations Organisation to differentiate between the nations of sovereign status, which are its direct members and organisations that collaborated with or received grants from its agencies to implement development programmes.

Many CSOs find themselves uncomfortable with this definition. It is argued that this gives a negative description of their not being a part of government establishment, and is also silent about organisation, ideology, functions, goals and jurisdiction.

CSOs are no more voluntary agencies because the direction of the organisations is dictated largely by availability of funds, and the character of programmes, priorities and objectives of the sponsors.

Now CSOs are considered as institutions and structures of people's participation in development activities which can be as variedly channelised as they are people centred. From the individual based organisations, forum networks are emerging with mutual working relationships.

Role and Dynamics of Civil Society Organisations

CSOs and Development

Development being people centred, participation of people in various interfaces is a prime requisite for success. The participation in development process has to cover areas of decision making, plan formulation, implementation, monitoring and evaluation.

Realising the need for participation of people in development process, Government of India acknowledged the role of Civil Society Organisations in the fields of education, health and social services while drafting VI Five Year Plan (1980 – 85). VI Five Year Plan identified new areas in which CSOs participation was envisaged. Broad areas of participation are:

1. Optimal utilization and development of renewable sources of energy including forestry through formation of renewals energy associations at the block level.
2. Family welfare, health and nutrition, education and relevant community programmes in the field.
3. Health for all programmes.
4. Water management and soil conservation.
5. Social welfare programmes for weaker sections.
6. Minimum needs programmes.
7. Disaster preparedness and management.
8. Promotional ecology and tribal development.
9. Environment protection and education.

CSOs – Cost Effective Functionaries

CSOs enjoy some distinct advantages in their functioning as cost effective functionaries viz.:-

- Proximity to people, flexibility, spirit of service
- Ability to motivate the people
- Ability to pave way for more decentralized, democratic and less bureaucratized administration of development.
- Through their empathy they can build awareness in people and train to trouble shoot.
- They can design programmes for target groups.
- Their flexible and informal delivery system is highly cost effective.

☞ They are best suited to bring about social change and proactive action.

CSOs and Enterprise Development in Rural Areas

Though almost 60 to 70% of the population in India depends on agriculture for its livelihood, agricultural sector contributes only 30% to National Income which evidence the low levels of productivity and underemployment in this sector. A large portion of worker force can be redeployed in non-farm sector without affecting productivity in agricultural sector.

The challenge posed before CSOs is how to take full advantage of environment that the government has created through formulation of policies and schemes that are helpful to the poor, particularly the rural poor. CSOs have to create linkages between the institutions and people so as to empower the poor to take advantage of resources available in the environment and the incentives provided by government as part of its development plans.

Enterprise development enables the poor to stand on their own feet. Government and Civil Society Organisations have to play a mutually complementary role in promoting enterprises. Up-gradation of professional skills, entrepreneurial motivation and management skills being the basic inputs to setup an enterprise.

Contemporary Scenario Abroad

- Governments in developed and developing countries over the world recognize that development cannot be brought about on its own. It is realized that the role of government is to create a conducive social, economic and political environment in which development may take place through a mixture of pubic and private institutions. Sustainable development is perceived as a shared institutional responsibility of government and civil society.

With the exception of United Kingdom, no other country has depended so heavily on voluntary sector to perform as many public activities as the United States. Private action is seen as primary market for societal development and at times for political influence.

CSOs also have an important research function which is rarely acknowledged and poorly supported in India. CSOs are projected as valuable laboratories for public health, credit for the poor, women emancipation, child labour, environmental issues and a wide range of other activities in UK and USA.

US Experience

American CSOs are popularly called as PVOs (private voluntary organisations). The international development of PVO community emerged from a missionary and humanitarian tradition as a response to enormous needs following World Wars I and II.

UK – The Oldest Model

The development of CSO community in United Kingdom is one of the strongest and oldest worldwide. Many of today's popular church based CSOs began as part of UK missionary efforts in the last century. Save the Children Fund (SCF), began after World War I and Oxfams started in 1942 as a response to Greek famine.

Norway – Setting Trends In CSO Movement

Today Norway is a nation with thousands of voluntary organisations many of which have strong ties both financial and otherwise, with some level of government. It is said that most Norwegians belong to at least two or three voluntary organisations.

Norway has been innovative example of organized public and fund receiving campaign. The largest is an annual television campaign known as television collection. Each year sponsoring television company selects an CSO or a group of CSOs along with a campaign theme for an intensive one day public appeal. The campaign receives active support from government and the royal family.

Canada–Funding Through CIDA

Canadian International Development Agency is responsible for the management of 75% of Canadian development assistance budget.

Canada's development assistance programme is based on a development charter "sharing our future" adopted in 1987. The charter's four main principles are to help the world's poorest countries and people to strengthen the human and institutional capacity of developing countries to solve their own problems in harmony with their national environment development priorities to prevail over other foreign policy goals and to strengthen the links between Canadian citizens and institutions and those in the third world.

Germany–Large Numbers and Political Foundations Too

CSO community in Germany is large, comprising some 2000 national and local groups, of which approximately 150 receive government financial support. The ten largest raise approximately 60 per cent of all public donations for international development work.

CSOs community can be divided into four different groups: the church related, non-confessional, local groups and the political foundations.

The political foundations in Germany are a unique feature of European CSO scenario. Each is affiliated to a political party. Foundation resources are 100 per cent government since they are prohibited from fund raising.

Main actively of political foundation is political education and in this they seek cooperation of trade unions, political parties, employer organisations, cooperatives and youth organisations. These foundations also promote self-help organisations particularly in rural areas. They are also involved in mass media promotion and research projects.

The Netherlands – Promoting Common Policy Culture

The Netherlands government has developed a special co-financing arrangement which envisages close cooperation between CFO and government at a policy level with clear objectives of improving the lot of the poor as:

- ☞ To contribute to the application of human rights.
- ☞ To strengthen participation of the poor in the development of their societies.
- ☞ To alleviate poverty and to contribute to the self-reliance of the poor.

Government's Initiatives for Growth of CSOs

1960	Freedom from Hunger Programme – culminating in formation of voluntary agency, People's Action for Development India (PADI). Modest beginning for involving CSOs in rural development programmes.
1977	Planning Commission constituted a committee under the chairmanship of Mr. B. Sivaraman to evolve a strategy for active and meaningful participation of voluntary agencies in rural development. It submitted a report of recommendations in 1978.
1978	Amendment to/provision in Income Tax Act Section 35 CCC (1977) Central Income Tax Act. National Adult Education Programme NAEP.
1978-79	Integrated Rural Development Programme (IRDP). Training of rural youth for self-employment (TRYSEM).

1980 National Rural Employment Programme.

1982-83 Development of Women & Children in Rural Areas (DWCRA).

1981-82 CSOs involved in selection and training of honorary rural organisations

1982 Consultative groups of CSOs for implementation of schemes under 20-point programme.

1983 CSOs involved in identification, release and rehabilitation of bonded labour.

1984 Mr. Bunker Roy appointed as consultant to Planning Commission on voluntary agencies.

1985 Seventh Five Year Plan – a section on voluntary agencies was included.

Government proposed a code of conduct for agencies seeking government funds.

Rs.150 crore allocations made for distribution to CSOs through CAPART

1986 CAPART formed by merging PADI & CART, the main objective being, to promote and assist voluntary action in the implementation of rural projects.

CAPART encouraged voluntary efforts on injecting new techniques.

(*Source*: Course material for Post Graduation Diploma In Rural Management (RDD-5), The Indira Gandhi National Open University School of Continuing Education, New Delhi).

Activities of CSOs in India

Present Range, Problems, Challenges

The activities of CSOs in India have become so diverse and multifaceted that any attempt to label one organisation with an activity would not be in right spirit. There was been a proliferation of non-governmental organisations in India across the country each with its specific perspectives, priorities and strategies. Geographically the growth of CSOs has not been uniform. The reason for such disparity was the non-availability of infrastructural facilities. Some organisations are multi-sectoral or integrated in their approach. It is also quite possible to find different types of voluntary organisations carrying out some sectoral work in the same areas but having totally different orientation, approach and activities. Thus the process of an organisation mainly depended on the strategy of intervention.

Over the last two decades, non-governmental organisations have been successful in engaging government in policy debate even on issues hither to ignored like legal rights, deforestation, sustainable development, women's oppression, etc. Every CSO is making a concerted effort in some activity or the other aimed at poverty alleviation in rural and urban areas. Success stories in each state and region are interlaced with problems of survival and sustainability.(Hann, C. and Dumn, E. 1996)

CSO movement in its journey with the active partnership of government and funding agencies has taken three directions namely:

- Grass-root CSOs, native in character and local-specific.
- Professional CSOs, having structured organisations with resource funding and well trained functionaries engaged in systematic approach, implementation and monitoring of programmes.
- Consultant and support CSOs, which in turn promote finance and support self-help beneficiary groups/small CSO groups in areas not accessible to them.

Sectors of Activities

Taking an overview of the operation of various CSOs across the country, the following major sectors can be mentioned:

1 Social awareness
2 Economic development
3 Environmental issues
4 Health care services
5 Non-formal education
6 Social forestry
7 Non-conventional energy sources
8 Water management
9 Vocational training
10 Dissemination of technology
11 Income generating activities
12 Legal Aid
13 Women development
14 Child issues
15 Helping aged/disabled

Sub-Classification of Sectors

I. Education:

A. Non-formal adult education

B. Formal education for school dropouts.

II. Child Development:

A. Nutrition programmes

B. Creche programme

C. Integrated activities under balwadi programme

D. Holiday camps for children.

III. Women Development:

A. Women awareness programme

B. Homes for girls/destitutes

C. Eradication of social evils (dowry/child marriage,

alcoholism/ prostitution/ drug abuse/smoking/ superstitions, etc.)

D. Income Generating Activities

IV. Health:

A. Vaccination programme

B. Blood camps

C. Awareness programme on family planning, AIDS etc

D. Eye camps

E. Free medical aid

F. Nutrition programme

G. Drinking water schemes.

V. Environment:

A. Ecology and environment awareness

B. Environment conservation

C. Social forestry

- Tree plantation, horticulture, waste land development

VI. Non-conventional Energy Sources:

A. Biogas technology promotion

B. Construction of improved chullahs.

VII. Rural Sanitation Programmes:

A. Construction of low cost latrines

B. Sanitation awareness.

VIII. Rural Housing:

A. Promotion of low cost houses through technology

B. Group housing

IX. Animal Husbandry:

A. Dairy/goat rearing/sheep rearing/rabbit rearing/ sericulture/ apiary.

X. Watershed management:

A. Irrigation tanks

B. Rainwater harvesting.

XI. Promotion of Local Crafts:

A. Handicrafts, pottery, drafting, etc.

XII. Micro Finance:

A. Formation of credit/saving group

B. Self-help groups (SHGs)

C. Financing SHGs.

XIII. Computer Training:

A. Awareness programme

B. Training programme.

XIV. Legal Aid:

A. Free legal consultation

B. Free professional services.

XV. Vocational training:

A. Tailoring/toy making, etc.

B. Skill development programmes for artisans.

XVI. Agriculture Supportive Programmes:

A. Cold storage facilities

B. Warehouse facilities.

XVII. Rehabilitation Programmes:

A. Refugee rehabilitation

B. Victim of natural disasters

C. Socially and Physically challenged.

XVIII. Marketing of Produce:

A. Training programmes

B. Arranging linkages.

XIX. Family Counselling

XX. CSO Consultancy

Dilemmas of CSOs in India

In the wake of failure to develop a clear demarcation of role of indigenous CSOs, the search to identify CSOs is still continuing. Management and organizational deficiencies reflect the infancy stage of many CSOs at grassroot level in rural development.

- The mushrooming growth of local CSOs and unhealthy competition for resources has contributed to cynicism and negative attitude in public thus affecting the credentials of voluntary service.
- Majority of CSOs are small in number and lack trained staff for their projects. CSOs are unable to retain efficient workers due to low pay and inability to guarantee future security. Communication and transport constraints in rural areas continue to hamper activities of CSOs.
- CSOs have few resources for project preparation, base line data collection, appraisal, monitoring and evaluation. Some projects with inadequate funding remain incomplete leading to the problem of sustainability.
- At present there is no system through which an upcoming CSO can establish its credentials for resource mobilization.

Challenges before CSOs

- Strive to influence the government to regard CSOs as valued development agencies in their own right and not simply as a delivering mechanism like other government department.

- Establishment of suitable mechanism that safeguards interests of CSOs on a continuing basis.
- Evolving uniform parameters of performance for funding and standardizing institutional evaluation.
- Promoting umbrella organisations as representatives of its members.
- Creating a platform for mutual understanding and forging regional alliances among local CSOs.
- Strengthening the capacity of CSOs to understand the local needs, problems and resources, to experiment with new programmes and strategies for development.
- Creating a professional work culture for CSOs.

Performance Constraints

- Many CSOs have chosen to undertake development work along regional lines. This has resulted in lack of wider perspective in thinking and clarity about impact of activity.
- Proliferation of CSOs in some regions has been creating a negative perception about CSOs movement. Failure to develop a clear demarcation of indigenous CSOs roles and functions has compounded the problem resulting in identity crisis. There are instances of misunderstanding between local CSOs and linkages such as government authorities and donor agencies over the methodology of implementation of schemes.
- Due to deficient infrastructural facilities like transportation, many CSOs operate from semi urban and urban areas for the rural projects.
- Total dependence on external funding resulting in donor driven activities and programmes rather than need based programmes.

- Failure to develop grassroot linkages with agencies/ government departments.
- Many CSOs do not have adequate administrative capacity for implementation of projects. Being small in resources and size, many CSOs are not able to arrange training for their field staff. Even after training, it is becoming increasingly difficult for small CSOs to retain the staff due to low salaries and inability to guarantee future security, as CSOs themselves are not sure about flow of funds from donor agencies.
- Funding is still a major problem and many CSOs are perpetually running short of funds. Financial institutions are yet to simplify their procedures and terms of finance to CSOs. Some projects are insufficiently funded leading to the problem of sustainability.
- Due to illiteracy among beneficiaries, in the initial stages CSOs are facing hostility and resistance.
- Lack of coordination and expertise sharing among CSOs operating in the same area.
- At present there is no system of developing CSOs through training. As a result larger assistance is still being routed through better known and established CSOs.
- System of credit rating of CSOs is not uniform and parameters of ratings are not standardized.
- Appraisal process of projects is bogged down by inordinate procedural blocks and bureaucratic indifference towards CSOs.
- Lack of empathy on the part of government officials with CSOs on their methodology of operation and cost of overheads.
- Political interference to comer benefits through CSOs because of their vested interests.

- Women CSOs are severally challenged by the constraints of shortage of skilled and educated women in the local areas. Further women CSOs are also faced with specific challenges that are gender related.
- Due to funding and accountability stipulations made by donor agencies and government, CSOs select a non-controversial area of operation. These programmes may succeed only in similar socio-economic cultural settings are not conducive to encouraging speedier innovative practices.

3

Human Resource Management and Change Management Practices in Civil Society Organisations

The leadership of any organization plays a crucial and decisive role in fulfilling its purpose. Recent years have seen the mushrooming of a lot of organizations in the voluntary sector, created by people who have seen easy ways of making money for themselves from the aid created by donors, or by those who have no other opportunities for their livelihood. The leadership of voluntary organizations demands a high level of vision and imagination, combined with a sense of missionary zeal. It is rather sad to see that the growing numbers of CSOs are marked more by the lack of such leadership than by its presence.

An equally important requirement of CSOs in the future will be to run them on highly professional lines, not dissimilar to the way profit-oriented organizations are managed. This demands that CSOs are managed by professionals. Given, however, the size of many CSOs and their limited vision, it is doubtful whether they will be able to afford to hire and retain professional managers to manage their operations.

CSOs can be classified on the basis of their size, activities, scale of operation, source of origin or use of professional inputs in the organization.

Source : OD in NGO sector, SEARCH BULLETIN, Volume VI June –Aug 2003. *(For Details see Table 3.1 to 3.4)*

Table 3.1: Criteria for classification of CSOs (Size)

Size	*V.small*	*Small*	*Medium*	*Large*	*V.Large*
Villages Covered	<10	11-30	31-100	Block	Several Blocks
					One/many districts
No.of Staff Employeed	<6	<15	<30	<100	101-1000
Volume of Funds(Rs)	<1 Lakhs	5-10 Lakhs	50 Lakhs to 1 Crore	1 Crore plus	Multi Crores

Source : OD in NGO sector, *Search Bulletin,* Volume VI June –Aug 2003

Table 3.2: Criteria for classification of CSOs (Activity)

Generic	Mobilisation, Implementing Govt.schemes Welfare Programmes
Sectoral Activities	Health, Agriculture, Economic development, Women's Development, Tribal Development, etc.
Multi Sectoral Activities	Health, Agriculture, Women's Development, Ecology
Support Services	Training, Research, Evaluation, Development publications etc.

Source: OD in NGO sector, *Search Bulletin,* Volume VI June –Aug 2003

Similarly, the activities undertaken by different CSOs across states illustrated in Table 3.5 elucidate the mainstreaming efforts of CSOs. It shows that more than 50% of the CSOs are involved in mainstream development activities such as, integrated rural development, health, women and children's development, environmental development and education. This manifests the propound interest of CSOs to perform the mainstream development roles. This also qualifies the CSOs to become a third sector. Focus on women and

Table 3.3: Criteria for classification of CSOs (Source of origin)

- Gandhian Background
- Marxist Background
- J P Movement
- Church Background
- Professional Background (e.g., Medical Doctors, Environmental Scientists, Management Graduates, Professional Social workers Exploring alternatives to reach the poor.)

Source : OD in NGO sector, *Search Bulletin,* Volume VI June –Aug 2003

Table 3.4: Criteria for Classification of CSOs (Professional Inputs)

Inputs	*Present(P)/ Absent(A)*
Subject Matter Specialist :	
1. Agriculture Scientists	P/A
2. Hydrologists	P/A
3. Animal husbandry specialists	P/A
4. Medical Doctors	P/A
5. Gender Specialists	P/A
6. Management Specialists	P/A
7. Social Scientists/ Professional Social workers	P/A
8. Researchers	P/A
9. Documentationists	P/A
10. Charted Accountants/Commerce Graduates	P/A
11. Computer System specialists	P/A

Source: OD in NGO Sector, *Search Bulletin,* Volume VI June–Aug 2003.

children tend to be prominent in most of the organizations, along with the other mainstream activities. Interestingly, campaigns and advocacy roles were under taken by a large number of CSOs.

Moreover, the budgetary trend indicates that a large chunk of the organization reminded small, while only 5% of the organizations grew to become big with a budget of more than a crore. In other words, since the organizations in their initial stages tend to be small, only 60% of the organizations graduate to medium size and around 10% become mega organizations. The rest of 30% either remain as small, without any scaling up efforts or quit from the development intervention. It manifests that only 70% of the organizations make scaling up efforts and only 10% succeeds in becoming big CSOs. The rest of the CSOs disappear after being there for a decade or two. Thus, the sustainability in CSOs is a snake and ladder game.

Women empowerment, health and education tend to dominate the development works of CSOs. Though these are social components, the approach followed in these, remains to be economic, such as micro-credit programmes and community resource management. Training as an activity tends to display its prominence because of internal trainings.

Responses of Managements of CSOs on HRM and Change Management in their Organisations

This being the overall situation of CSOs with respect to the CSOs functioning country wide, a study was conducted on a random sample of 225 of CSOs working for the past 10 years in the state of Andhra Pradesh. These organizations represented various geographical locations, various reference groups and different fields of activity in the state. The study was conducted through a questionnaire, responses obtained and the data was analysed and presented as followed.

Profile of CSOs

On the whole 225 CSOs were selected for present study. Almost all of them have more than 10 years of existence in their respective field of activities.

Background of the founders

When the Background of the Founders of Organisations was probed, it showed that they were with different background in the sense that they were from educational, social service, industrial, retired public servants etc. About 42% of the Founders of CSOs were with social service background, followed by the background of the retired public servants (24%), educational service (23%) and with industrial background(about 10%).

Focus areas of activity

The sample CSOs were broadly categorised by their area of activity. Majority of the CSOs (26%) were working on Dalit issues, followed by Women and gender issues (24%), Tribal related issues (23%) and on issue of Children (10%), Rural development (9%), Youth related issues (6%) and the rest on other focus areas.

Ideology of the organisations

On the basis of the ideology of the organizations the sample CSOs were framed into 3 main ideologies, namely, Marxian, Gandhian and Socialist. Among the sample CSOs 54% were following Gandhian ideologies,31% were based on Socialist ideologies and 14% were having Marxian ideologies.

Ideology and focus area of activity

When we examined the ideology of the organization and the focus area of activity, it was observed that CSOs with Gandhian ideology were focusing on issues related to tribals, Dalits and Rural People. On the other hand Organisations with Socialist and Marxian ideology on concentrating on areas relating to Women, Children and Youth.

Mission Statement

As regards mission statement for the organizations, 56% of the sample CSOs were having and the rest of them reportedly did not have the mission statement. On the basis of Ideology, the percentage of organizations having mission statement was higher in Socialist Ideology when compared to organizations with Gandhian Ideologies. By focused areas of organizations, almost all the organizations working in Rural Development, Children and Youth related issues were having mission statements. Among the Organisations which were focusing on Tribal, Dalit and Gender issues, many of them do not have any such mission statements (below 50% the CSOs in their respective fields were reportedly having mission statements).

Organisational Objectives (Founder's Background-wise)

The Data collected from the sample CSOs was classified based on Founder's Background (Educational, Social service, Industrialist, Retired from service and others) and parameters like Organisational goals, Objectives, Functioning of the Organisation, the approach followed by the organizations etc were examined and details were as followed. (For details see Table 3.5)

The statement "Every organisation should have goals to function effectively", almost all of them (96%) agreed upon, irrespective of their ideologies and focused area of activities. When we examine the degree of agreement 43% of them just agreed, 31% of them moderately agreed, about 22% of them strongly agreed.

With respect to the statement "Every organisation should have objectives to achieve the goals", out of 225 sample CSOs 207 were in agreement with the statement amounting to 92%, whereas only 18 were of the negative opinion amounting to 8%.

In response to the statement "Functioning of the organisation depends on the motto with which we are working",

Table 3.5: Responses of Managements of CSOs on Organisational Objectives (Founder's Background wise)

(In percentages)

S.No	Statement	SA	A	MA	Total Agreed	MD	SD	Total Disagreed	Total
1	Every organisation should have goals to function effectively	22	43	31	96	4	0]	4	100
2	Every organisation should have objectives to achieve the goals	21	40	70	92	7	1	8	100
3	Functioning of the organisation depends on the motto with which we are working	16	43	32	90	9	1	10	100
4	We are working strictly in line with the objectives set out at the time of Incorporation of the organisation	18	46]	26	90	9.5	0.5	10	100
5	Organisational success depends on adapting to new challenges every time instead of a Consistency approach	23	40	30	93	6.5	0.5	7	100
6	Activities are mere activities. They should also be used as strategies to achieve the goals	24	45	22	92	7	1	8	100

Source: Primary Data

about 16% strongly agreed, 43% just agreed, 32% moderately agreed amounting to 90% of the responses given in the affirmative.

With regard to the statement on "We are working strictly in line with the objectives set out at the time of Incorporation of the organization", about 90% of the respondents were of the opinion that their organizations were working strictly in line with objectives set out at the beginning.

When we examined the responses on the statement "Organisational success depends on adapting to new challenges every time instead of a Consistency approach", about 40% just agreed followed by 30% who moderately agreed and 18% strongly agreed, totaling 90% of responses on the positive side.

Organisational Objectives (Founder's Background-wise)

When the question of activities being used as strategies to achieve Organisational Objectives was put to the respondents through the statement "Activities are mere activities. They should also be used as strategies to achieve the goals", 24% strongly agreed, 45% just agreed and 22% moderately agreed.

When the aspect of Change of Activities over the period was examined about 125 respondents said that there was change, where as 100 respondents said "No", indicating that a slight majority of the organizations had been shifting the areas of activities over the period.

The overall perception of the respondents for all the statements regarding Organisational Objectives had been on the agreement side with more than 90% of the respondents agreeing to the statements.

Internal Management (Founder's Background-wise)

While looking into internal Management Particulars the decision-making process in the organization, we have examined whether the decision-making process is involved

Table 3.6: Responses of Managements of CSOs on Internal Management and Decision-making regarding HRM (Founder's Background-wise)

(In percentage)

S.NO	*Major Decision*	*Centralised*	*BoG*	*CC*	*All Staff*	*Ad hoc*	*Total*
1	Planning of Activities	61.5	22.5]	13	1	2	100
2	Implementation process for activities	18	50	25	5.5	0.5	100
3	Major Focus Shift	22.5	38.5	27	6	7	100
4	Financial Decisions	22	43	20	10	5	100
5	Monitoring of Activities	19	30	35	7	9	100
6	Employee recruitment	23.5	35	24	10	7.5	100
7	Promotions of employees	16	41	24	11	8	100
8	Pay Hike / Incentives to employees	19.5	35.5	29	9	7	100
9	Performance Appraisals	22.5	31	28.5	11	7	100
10	Staff Monitoring	24	35	23	9	9	100
11	Problem solving	23	34	28	7	8	100
12	Liaisoning and Promotional activities	36	25	23	8	8	100

Source : Primary Data

with members of the organization ranging from Board of Governors to all staff or Centralised Leadership. It gives an idea of whether the decision making process is centralized or decentralized.

Major decision making process with respect to 'Planning of activities of the organization', majority (62%) of the organizations were in favour of the centralized decision making by the head of organization, followed by decision making involved with Board of Governors (23%) and the core committee (13%). The involvement of ground level activists in the decision making process is negligible across the organizations irrespective of the background of their founder.

Another decision making activity with respect to 'Implementation process for activities', about 50% of the organizations responded that Board of Governors of the organizations decide on implementation process followed by core committee (25%) and centralized leadership (18%).

With respect to decision making on 'Major focus shift', in 22.5% of the organizations centralised leadership or head of the organization decided where as in majority of the organizations, specific decision making groups like Board of Governors (38.5%) and core committees (27%) were involved in decision making leaving little room for ground level activists.

When decision making process regarding 'Financial Decisions' in the organizations was examined in 43% of the organizations Board of Governors took decisions, followed by 22% by centralized leadership, 20% by the core committee. Though there were responses that all staff (10%) and Ad-hoc committees (5%) would take Financial Decisions, the argument was not tenable and it had to be probed further.

With regarding to 'Monitoring of Activities' as a part of internal management, 35% of the organizations responded that core committee would monitor, followed by Board of Governors (30%), centralized leadership (19%) and Ad-hoc committees (9%).

Internal Management and Decision-making (Founder's Background-wise)

When the decision-making process regarding 'Employee Recruitment' was examined, in 35% of the organizations it was reportedly done by Board of Governors (35%), core committee (25%) and centralized leadership (23.5%). There were some responses from organizations that all staff (10%) and Ad-hoc committees (7.5%) would also decide on employee recruitment.

Another major decision making process about 'Promotion of Employees' as a part of internal management in the organization, again Board of Governors played a major role in 41% of the organizations followed by core committees (24%) and centralized leadership (16%). In some organizations (about 19%), all staff and Ad-hoc committees (appointed for the purpose) were reportedly involved.

With respect to internal management decision on 'Pay hike / Incentives to Employees', as an integral part of Human Resource Management, in about 40% of the organizations Board of Governors, in 29% core committees and in about 20% centralized leadership would take the decisions. In about 9% of the organizations all staff were involved in decision making regarding pay hike and incentives.

When the decision-making activity regarding 'Performance Appraisals' was examined 31% of the respondents said that it would taken by Board of Governors followed by core committee (28.5%), Centralised leadership (22.5%), all staff (11%) and Ad-hoc committees (7%).

When the organistions was questioned as to who would 'Monitor Staff', Board of Governors were reportedly taking decisions in 35% of the organizations followed by centralized leadership or Head of the Oraganisation (24%), core committee (23%), Ad-hoc committee (9%) and all staff (9%).

When it came to 'Problem Solving' as a Human Resource Management activity in the organizations, in majority of them it was done by Board of Governors (34%), followed by core committees (28%), Centralised Leadership (22%), Ad-hoc committees (8%). Some organizations (7%) responded that all staff were involved in problem solving activities in order to ensure delegation and decentralization of decision making and to reduce bias and prejudice.

With respect to 'Liaisoning and Promotional Activities' for the organizations, in about 36% of the organizations it was reportedly handling the centralized leadership, followed by Board of Governors (25%), Core committee (23%), all staff (8%) and Ad-hoc committees (8%). Though some respondents claimed that all staff were involved in 'Liaisoning and Promotional Activities', it was not practically possible.

The decision making process in CSOs is quite complicated as the governance structures in the organization transcend their boundaries. The boundary management in the organizations became perplexing. The leader's presence is conspicuous in all decisions, though the decisions go in the name of concerned structures. The decision-making process is analysed by looking into the liaisoning decisions, major focus shift, financial decisions, monitoring activities, staff appraisal and staff monitoring.

The important structures for governance commonly are leaders, the Board, core team and staff member teams. An analysis of the functioning of these structures in the selected organizations is presented.

Recruitment (Founder's Background-wise)

As a part of Human Resource Management in Civil Society Organisations the researcher examined the view points on recruitment and the following table indicates the responses given on aspects relating to recruitment of employees. (For Details see Table No 3.7)

With respect to the statement "Recruitment of employees in the organisation should be based on policies such as gender

Table 3.7: Responses of Managements of CSOs on Recruitment of employees (Founder's Background-wise)

(In percentage)

S.No.	*Statement*	*SA*	*A*	*MA*	*Total Agreed*	*MD*	*SD*	*Total Disagreed*	*Total*
1	Recruitment of employees in the organisation should be based on policies such as gender proportion, Caste proportion	23	31	31	86	10	4	14	100
2	Employees should be recruited based on Competency alone	11	35	24	70	18.5	11.5	30	100
3	Qualified Specialist staff are helpful for the organisation	10	29	24	63	25]	12	37	100
4	Experienced Generalist staff are useful for the organisation	22	39	28	89	7	3	10	100

Source : Primary Data

proportion, Caste proportion", 31% Just agreed and 31% moderately agreed followed by 23% Strongly Agreed. It was also noticed that there was a disagreement regarding the statement from 14% of the respondents.

When the statement "Employees should be recruited based on Competency alone" was examined, about 70% of the respondents were in agreement by saying that competency alone should be considered for recruitment, where as the rest of 30% of the respondents felt that competence alone would not be sufficient.

With regard to statement "Qualified Specialist staff are helpful for the organisation", there was not much uniformity in thinking when it was observed 63% of the respondents felt that qualified specialist staff would helpful, where as 37% of the respondents were vehemently opposing giving an indication that specific task masters suite only to the specific tasks would not help the organisation in the long run.

As a supporting argument, when the statement "Experienced Generalist staff are useful for the organisation" was examined 89% of the respondents were in agreement and only 10% of the respondents opposed. It clearly showed that experienced staff with general skills would be helpful for the organisation to meet the long term objectives of the organisation.

Recruitment (Founder's Background-wise)

When the aspect of how the man power required for the organisation was examined it was found that organisations were accessing staff through various sources. In about 38% of the organisations, the prospective employees were said to approach directly asking for jobs, 27% of the staff were reportedly recruited through reference from others, 14% of the staff were reportedly recruited on spotting the employees working in other organisations and inviting them to join. Apart from these traditional sources of recruitment some organisations were reportedly drawing manpower from the market through recruitment consultants (11%) and Newspaper advertisement (10%). It was observed that recruitment process was slowly becoming market-driven and competence-oriented.

Except the fact that there was a greater degree of disagreement on the statements that "employees should be recruited based on competence alone" and "qualified specialist staff are helpful for the organisation", on other statements the respondents were almost in complete agreement with them.

Motivation (Founder's Background-wise)

For Organisations to sustain over a period and for better Human Resource Management motivation of the employees is one of the factors. The perception of the managements of CSOs on employee motivation in their respective organizations was examined by the researcher. (For Details see Table No 3.8)

In response to the statement "Retaining Employees in the organisation is becoming difficult", a total of 85% of the respondents were in agreement with 15% opposing it. When we examined the details 36% had just agreed to the statement, 33% moderately agreed, followed by 16% strongly agreed. It indicated that retention of employees in CSOs had become a tough task for the managements.

With respect to the statement "We are remunerating the employees according to their Competency / Skills / Qualifications", the perception of the respondents was: 39% moderately agreed, 28% just agreed, 12% strongly agreed and on the other side 15% of the respondents moderately disagreed and 6% of them strongly disagreed. If we broadly take the positive and negative responses into consideration, 79% were on the positive side and 21% are on the negative side, which indicated that some management of CSOs confessed to the fact that they were not remunerating the employee properly.

With regard to the statement "Financial benefits motivate

Table 3.8: Details showing the responses of Managements of CSOs on Motivation of employees (Founder's Background wise).

(In percentage)

S.No	Statement	SA	A	MA	Total Agreed	MD	SD	Total Disagreed	Total
1	Retaining Employees in the organisation is becoming difficult	16	36	33	85	12	3	15	100
2	We are remunerating the employees according to heir Competency / Skills/ Qualifications	12	28	39	79	15	6	21	100
3	Financial benefits motivate the employee more than intrinsic benefits	12	31.5	35.5	79	17	4	21	100

Source : Primary Data

the employee more than intrinsic benefits", 35.5% of the respondents moderately agreed, followed by 31.5% just agreed, 12% strongly agreed. On the other side of the argument about 21% of the respondents disagreed to the statement and felt that financial benefits alone would not matter, but other intrinsic benefits like appreciation of the work done by the employee, recognition of the potential of the employee etc would also matter to motivate the employees for better performance.

In service organisations like CSOs commitment of the staff to the cause had to be at the highest level. Unike in Government and Private sector organisations, employees in CSOs were expected to have commitment to the cause which was been pursued by the managements. In response to the statement "Commitment of our staff to the cause is: " 55% of the respondents felt moderate, 24% below average, 17% high,4% low. Therefore majority of the managements of the organizations were not convinced about the commitment of their staff.

On the whole, the respondents were of the opinion that retention of employees in the organizations was difficult despite financial benefits, which could never be given according to the expectations of the employees.

Training and Development (Founder's Background-wise)

In Human Resource Management of any organization training and development is one of the important components. The researcher attempted to find the perceptions of managements of CSOs on training and development with respect to their organizations. (For Details see Table No 3.9)

In response to the statement "Training should be given to both fresh and experienced people" a total of about 82% of the respondents agreed and 18% were in disagreement. If we examine the details 30% just agreed, 40% moderately agreed and 12% strongly agreed; where as on the disagreement side 14% moderately disagreed and 4% of the respondents

Table 3.9: Responses of Managements of CSOs on Training & Development (Founder's Background-wise)

(In percentage)

S.No	*Statement*	*SA*	*A*	*MA*	*Total Agreed*	*MD*	*SD*	*Total Disagreed*	*Total*
1	2	3	4	5	6	7	8	9	10
1	Training should be given to both fresh and experienced people	12	30	40	82	14	4	18	100
2	In-house Training is more useful than sending employees to other organisations	16	33	35	84	13	3	16	100
3	Retaining the employees for longer duration brings success to the organisation rather than turning them out periodically	15.5	27.5	41	84	13	3	16	100

Source : Primary Data

strongly disagreed. It could be seen that there were respondents in majority, who felt training was essential for both freshers and experienced people.

With respect to the statement "In-house Training is more useful than sending employees to other organisations", the respondents, irrespective of the background of the founder, moderately agreed (35%), agreed (33%), and strongly agreed (16%). There were also some opposing responses: Moderately disagreed (13%), strongly disagreed (3%). The overall impression of the respondents could be that In-house training was more useful for the employees than sending them to the other organisations for training.

In response to the statement "Retaining the employees for longer duration brings success to the organisation rather than turning them out periodically:" 41% of the respondents moderately agreed, 27.5% just agreed and 15.5% strongly agreed, totally 84% of the respondents agreed with the statement and 16% were in disagreement. Therefore retention of employees for a longer period in the organisation was reportedly giving success to the organisations, which ensures continuity in the activities both in quality and quantity.

With regard to the statement "Capacity Building for our staff is done in: " 42% of the respondents said that their staff were capacitated in field level activities and 39% of the respondents said they would train their staff in management aspects and 19% of them said that training would be given in administrative matters. Majority of them ie: 94 out of 225 respondents felt that capacity building of the staff should be one in field level activities.

As one of the management concepts, SWOT Analysis is done for any kind of activity in an organization for self assessment of the progress. When the respondents were probed whether SWOT Analysis was periodically done in their respective organizations 80% of them said "Yes", with 20% saying "No".

With regard to the responses of the respondents on Training and Development of employees in their respective organizations, on an average 17% of respondents were not in agreement in with the statements.

Leadership, Monitoring and Evaluation (Founder's Background-wise)

Providing good leadership, periodic monitoring and evaluation are a part of good Human Resource Management in an organization. These aspects were also examined by the researcher and the perceptions of the respondents were detailed below. (For Details see Table No 3.10)

With regard to the statement "For the success of the organisation, Leader alone is responsible:" 37% of the respondents agreed, followed by 30% moderately agreed and 20% strongly agreed, totalling 87% of the respondents in agreement with the statement and 13% in disagreement of the statement. It indicated that leadership of the organisation played a major role in the success of the organisation.

When the managements of the Civil Society Organisations were probed whether employee should be continuously monitored and a day to day basis with the statement "Employees should be continuously monitored rather than assigning tasks and allowing them to complete the tasks" 48% moderately agreed, 17% just agreed and 12% strongly agreed. On the disagreement side of the statement 19% moderately disagreed and 4% strongly disagreed. The over all perception was 77% agreed and 23% disagreed. It showed that the managements felt that employees need to monitored and evaluated on a continuous basis without leaving them to complete the tasks on their own by fixing their own timelines.

For the statement "Leader should always guide and advise rather than involve in all day to day affairs", when we examine the perceptions of the respondents 38% were in agreement moderately, 27% just agreed, 13% strongly agreed, which indicated that the leader should always operate in a broader

Table 3.10: Responses of Managements of CSOs on Leadership, Monitoring& Evaluation (Founder's Background-wise)

(In percentage)

S.No	*Statement*	*SA*	*A*	*MA*	*Total Agreed*	*MD*	*SD*	*Total Disagreed*	*Total*
1	For the success of the organisation, Leader alone is responsible	20	37	30	87	9	4	13	100
2	Employees should be continuously monitored rather than assigning tasks and allowing them to complete the tasks	12	17	48	77	18	5	23	100
3	Leader should always guide and advise rather than involve in all day to day affairs	13	27	38	78	18	4	22	100

Source : Primary Data

framework and guide and advise rather than involving in day to day affairs. It was felt that day to day governing matters relating to the organisation should be delegated and decentralised.

When it was examined how periodically the progress of staff was monitored in the respective organisations with the statement "In our organisation we monitor the progress of staff', 16% of the respondents said they would monitor annually, 31% said half-yearly, 30% said quarterly, 14% said monthly and 9% said fortnightly. When we take the over all perception, about 77% of the respondents said they would review the progress quarterly and above.

In response to the statement "Have you ever done cost effectiveness analysis of the activities" about 73% of the respondents said they would do cost effectiveness analysis of the activities. It could be seen that majority of the respondents were cost conscious and try to do activities in a cost effective manner.

With regard to the statements on Leadership, Monitoring and Evaluation of employees, the respondents were in agreement to the degree of more than 77%. Whereas the degree of disagreement was averaging 18%.

Organisational Communication (Founder's Background-wise)

Communication within the organization and among the employees was one of the aspects which was examined by the researcher.

When it was examined whether downward and upward communication channels were encouraged in the respective organizations with the statement "We encourage both downward and upward communication channels", 80% of the respondents said they would. It could be attributed to the fact that the size of the CSOs was small and manageable and hence communication channels could be encouraged both ways.

In response to the statement "Employees should be encouraged to have inter personal Communications / relations while working in an organisation" a total of about 89% of the respondents were in agreement with the statement and 11% were in disagreement. To be elaborate, 36% of the respondents just agreed, 31% moderately agreed and 20% strongly agreed.

It indicated that majority of the respondents were in favour of encouraging interpersonal communications/ relations in their respective organisations.

Organisational Objectives (Reference Group-wise)

The Data collected from the sample CSOs was classified based on Reference groups (Tribals, Dalits, Women, Children, Rural People, Youth and others) and parameters like Organisational goals, Objectives, Functioning of the Organisation, the approach followed by the organizations etc were examined and details were as followed (For Details see Table No 3.11)

The statement "Every organisation should have goals to function effectively", almost all of them(97%) agreed upon, irrespective of their ideologies and focused area of activities. When we examine the degree of agreement 44% of them just agreed, 31% of them moderately agreed, about 22% of them strongly agreed.

With respect to the statement "Every organisation should have objectives to achieve the goals", out of 225 sample CSOs 200 were in agreement with the statement amounting to 89%, where as only 25 were of the negative opinion amounting to 11%.

In response to the statement "Functioning of the organisation depends on the motto with which we are working", about 11.5% strongly agreed, 42.5% just agreed, 32% moderately agreed amounting to 86% of the responses given in the affirmative.

With regard to the statement on "We are working strictly

Table 3.11: Responses of Managements of CSOs on Organisational Objectives (Reference group-wise)

(In percentage)

S.No	*Statement*	*SA*	*A*	*MA*	*Total Agreed*	*MD*	*SD*	*Total Disagreed*	*Total*
1	Every organisation should have goals to function effectively	22	44	31	97	3	0	3	100
2	Every organisation should have objectives to achieve the goals	20	40	29	89	8	3	11	100
3	Functioning of the organisation depends on the motto with which we are working	11.5	42.5	32	86	12	2	14	100
4	We are working strictly in line with the objectives set out at the time of Incorporation of the organisation	14	46	27	87	11	3	14	100
5	Organisational success depends on adapting to new challenges every time instead of a Consistency approach	23	38	29	90	6.5	3.5	10	100
6	Activities are here activities. They should also be used as strategic to achieve the goals	21	45	22	88	8	4	12	100

Source : Primary Data

in line with the objectives set out at the time of Incorporation of the organization", about 87% of the respondents were of the opinion that their organizations were working strictly in line with objectives set out at the beginning.

When we examined the responses on the statement "Organisational success depends on adapting to new challenges every time instead of a Consistency approach", about 38% just agreed, followed by 29% who moderately agreed and 23% strongly agreed, totaling 90% of responses on the positive side.

When the question of activities being used as strategies to achieve Organisational Objectives was put to the respondents through the statement "Activities are mere activities. They should also be used as strategies to achieve the goals", 21% strongly agreed, 45% just agreed and 22% moderately agreed.

When the aspect of Change of Activities over the period was examined about 124 respondents said that there was change, where as 101 respondents said "No", indicating that a slight majority of the organizations had been shifting the areas of activities over the period.

The responses of the managements of the CSOs on organizational objectives were in agreement to the degree of more than 86% and only around 14% disagreed with the statements.

Internal Management (Reference Group-wise)

While looking into Internal Management Particulars the decision making process in the organization, we have examined whether the decision making process is involved with members of the organization ranging from Board of Governors to all staff or Centralised Leadership basing on reference group (Tribals, Dalits, Women, Children, Rural People, Youth and others). It gives an idea of whether the decision making process is centralized or decentralized. (For Details see Table No 3.12)

Table 3.12: Responses of Managements of CSOs on Internal Management and Decision Making regarding HRM (Reference group-wise)

(In percentage)

S.NO	Major Decision	Centralised	Bog	CC	All Staff	Ad hoc	Total
1	Planning of Activities	62	23	14	1.5	0.5	100
2	Implementation process for activities	18	50	26	5	1	100
3	Major Focus Shift	23	38	27	7	5	100
4	Financial Decisions	22	43	20	9	6	100
5	Monitoring of Activities	19	30	35	7	9	100
6	Employee recruitment	24	35	24	9.	8	100
7	Promotions of employees	16	42	24	10.5	7.5	100
8	Pay Hike / Incentives to employees	20	36	29	8	7	100
9	Performance Appraisals	23	31	28	10	8	100
10	Staff Monitoring	24	36	24	8	8	100
11	Problem solving	23	34	27	7	8	100
12	Liaisoning and Promotional activities	37	25	23.5	6.5	8	100

Source : Primary Data

Major decision making process with respect to 'Planning of activities of the organization', majority (62%) of the organizations were in favour of the centralized decision making by the head of organization, followed by decision making involved with Board of Governors(23%) and the core committee(14%). The involvement of ground level activists in the decision making process was negligible across the organizations irrespective of the reference group.

Another decision making activity with respect to 'Implementation process for activities', about 50% of the organizations responded that Board of Governors of the organizations decide on implementation process followed by core committee(26%) and centralized leadership(18%).

With respect to decision making on 'Major focus shift', in 23% of the organizations centralised leadership or head of the organization decided, where as in majority of the organizations, specific decision making groups like Board of Governors (38%) and core committees(27%) were involved in decision making leaving little room for ground level activists.

When decision making process regarding 'Financial Decisions' in the organizations was examined in 43% of the organizations Board of Governors took decisions, followed by 22% by centralized leadership, 20% by the core committee. Though there were responses that all staff (9%) and Ad-hoc committees (6%) would take Financial Decisions, the argument was not tenable and it had to be probed further.

With regarding to 'Monitoring of Activities' as a part of internal management, 35% of the organizations responded that core committee would monitor, followed by Board of Governors(30%), centralized leadership(19%) and Ad-hoc committees(9%).

When the decision making process regarding 'Employee Recruitment' was examined, in 35% of the organizations it was reportedly done by Board of Governors (35%), core committee (24%) and centralized leadership (24%). There were some responses from organizations that all staff (9%) and Ad-hoc committees (8%) would also decide on employee recruitment.

Another major decision making process about 'Promotion of Employees' as a part of internal management in the organization, again Board of Governors played a major role in 42% of the organizations followed by core committees(24%) and centralized leadership(16%). In some organizations (about 18%), all staff and Ad-hoc committees (appointed for the purpose) were reportedly involved.

With respect to internal management decision on 'Pay hike / Incentives to Employees', as an integral part of Human Resource Management, in about 36% of the organizations Board of Governors, in 29% core committees and in about 20% centralized leadership would take the decisions. In about 8% of the organizations all staff were involved in decision making regarding Pay hike and incentives.

When the decision making activity regarding 'Performance Appraisals' was examined 31% of the respondents said that it would taken by Board of Governors followed by core committee(28%), Centralised leadership (23%), all staff (10%) and Ad-hoc committees(8%).

When the organistions were questioned as to who would 'Monitor Staff', Board of Governors were reportedly taking decisions in 36% of the organizations followed by centralized leadership or Head of the Oraganisation (24%), core committee(24%), Ad-hoc committee(8%) and all staff (8%).

When it came to 'Problem Solving' as a Human Resource Management activity in the organizations, in majority of them it was done by Board of Governors(34%), followed by core committees(27%), Centralised Leadership(23%), Ad-hoc committees(8%). Some organizations (7%) responded that all staff were involved in problem solving activities in order to ensure delegation and decentralization of decision making and to reduce bias and prejudice.

With respect to 'Liaisoning and Promotional Activities' for the organizations, in about 37% of the organizations it was reportedly handling the centralized leadership, followed by Board of Governors (25%), Core committee (23.5%), all staff (6.5%) and Ad-hoc committees (8%). Though some respondents claimed that all staff were involved in 'Liaisoning and Promotional Activities', it was not practically possible.

It explicates that the leader's discretion tends to be prominent in all the areas of decision making though most of them go in the letterhead of Board or core team(Particularly in the financial decisions, staff monitoring, major focus shift and liaisoning decisions). The core team concentrates on planning, implementing and monitoring activities and staff monitoring as well as appraisal. All staff are involved in Planning, implementing and monitoring activities. Though it clearly indicates the boundaries of different structures, the overlapping of decision-making process to different structures manifests the conflicts or lack of clarity in the decision making in the CSOs sector. The leader's role in all the components in the decision making process highlights the involvement of the leader in the running of the organization.

Recruitment of Employees (Reference Group-wise)

As a part of Human Resource Management in Civil Society Organisations the researcher examined the view points on recruitment and the following table indicates the responses given on aspects relating to recruitment of employees. (For details see Table 3.13)

With respect to the statement "Recruitment of employees in the organisation should be based on policies such as gender proportion, Caste proportion", 31.5% Just agreed and 31.5% moderately agreed followed by 24% Strongly Agreed. It was also noticed that there was a disagreement regarding the statement from 13% of the respondents.

When the statement "Employees should be recruited based on Competency alone" was examined, about 74% of the

Table 3.13: Responses of Managements of CSOs on Recruitment of Employees (Reference group-wise)

(In percentage)

S.NO	Statement	SA	A	MA	Total Agreed	MD	SD	Total Disagreed	Total
1	Recruitment of employees in the organisation should be based on policies such as gender proportion, Caste proportion	24	31.5	31.5	87	10	7[3]	13	100
2	Employees should be recruited based on Competency alone	13.5	36	24.5	74	19	7	26	100
3	Qualified Specialist staff are helpful for the organisation	13	30	20	63	25	12	37	100
4	Experienced Generalist staff are useful for the organisation	23	39	28	90	7	3	10	100

Source : Primary Data

respondents were in agreement by saying that competency alone should be considered for recruitment, where as the rest of 26% of the respondents felt that competence alone would not be sufficient.

With regard to statement "Qualified Specialist staff are helpful for the organisation", there was not much uniformity in thinking when it was observed 63% of the respondents felt that qualified specialist staff would helpful, where as 37% of the respondents were vehemently opposing giving an indication that specific task masters suite only to the specific tasks would not help the organisation in the long run.

As a supporting argument, when the statement "Experienced Generalist staff are useful for the organisation" was examined 90% of the respondents were in agreement and only 10% of the respondents opposed. It clearly showed that experienced staff with general skills would be helpful for the organisation to meet the long term objectives of the organisation.

When the aspect of how the man power required for the organisation was examined it was found that organisations were accessing staff through various sources. In about 40% of the organisations, the prospective employees were said to approach directly asking for jobs, 21% of the staff were reportedly recruited through reference from others, 13% of the staff were reportedly recruited on spotting the employees working in other organisations and inviting them to join. Apart from these traditional sources of recruitment some organisations were reportedly drawing manpower from the market through recruitment consultants (13%) and Newspaper advertisement (13%). It was observed that recruitment process was slowly becoming market-driven and competence-oriented.

In relation to the statements on Recruitment of employees, majority of the respondents were in agreement ranging from 63% to 90%.

Motivation of Employees (Reference Group-wise)

For Organisations to sustain over a period and for better Human Resource Management motivation of the employees is one of the factors. The perception of the managements of CSOs on employee motivation in their respective organizations reference group wise (Tribals, Dalits, Women, Children, Rural People, Youth and others) was examined by the researcher. (For Details see Table No 3.14).

In response to the statement "Retaining Employees in the organisation is becoming difficult", a total of 85% of the respondents were in agreement with 15% opposing it. When we examined the details 36% had just agreed to the statement, 33% moderately agreed, followed by 16% strongly agreed. It indicated that retention of employees in CSOs had become a tough task for the managements.

With respect to the statement "We are remunerating the employees according to their Competency / Skills / Qualifications", the perception of the respondents was: 39% moderately agreed, 28% just agreed, 12% strongly agreed and on the other side 15% of the respondents moderately disagreed and 6% of them strongly disagreed. If we broadly take the positive and negative responses into consideration, 79% were on the positive side and 21% are on the negative side, which indicated that some management of CSOs confessed to the fact that they were not remunerating the employee properly.

With regard to the statement "Financial benefits motivate the employee more than intrinsic benefits", 35.5% of the respondents moderately agreed, followed by 32% just agreed, 11.5% strongly agreed. On the other side of the argument about 21% of the respondents disagreed to the statement and felt that financial benefits alone would not matter, but other intrinsic benefits like appreciation of the work done by the employee, recognition of the potential of the employee etc would also matter to motivate the employees for better performance.

Table 3.14: Responses of Managements of CSOs on Motivation of employees (Reference group-wise)

(In percentage)

S.No	*Statement*	*SA*	*A*	*MA*	*Total Agreed*	*MD*	*SD*	*Total Disagreed*	*Total*
1	Retaining Employees in the organisation is becoming difficult	16	36	33	85	12	3	15	100
2	We are remunerating the employees according to their Competency / Skills / Qualifications	12	28	39	79	15	6	21	100
3	Training should be given to both fresh and experienced people	11.5	32	35.5	79	17	4	21	100

Source : Primary Data

In service organisations like CSOs commitment of the staff to the cause had to be at the highest level. Unike in Government and Private sector organisations, employees in CSOs were expected to have commitment to the cause which was been pursued by the managements. In response to the statement "Commitment of our staff to the cause is." 53% of the respondents felt moderate, 29% below average, 11% high,7% low. Therefore majority of the managements of the organizations were not convinced about the commitment of their staff.

On the aspect of motivation of employees in the respective organizations, the respondents were in agreement to the degree of more than 79%, indicating that there were about 21% of the respondents in disagreement with the statements.

Training & Development (Reference group-wise)

In Human Resource Management of any organization training and development is one of the important components. The researcher attempted to find the perceptions of managements of CSOs on training and development on the basis of reference group (Tribals, Dalits, Women, Children, Rural People, Youth and others) with respect to their organizations. (For Details see Table No 3.18)

In response to the statement "Training should be given to both fresh and experienced people" a total of about 84% of the respondents agreed and 16% were in disagreement. If we examine the details 30% just agreed, 42% moderately agreed and 12% strongly agreed; where as on the disagreement side 15% moderately disagreed and 1% of the respondents strongly disagreed. It could be seen that there were respondents in majority, who felt training was essential for both freshers and experienced people.

With respect to the statement "In-house Training is more useful than sending employees to other organisations", the

Table 3.15: Responses of Managements of CSOs on Training & Development of Employees (Reference group-wise)

(In percentage)

S.No	Statement	SA	A	MA	Total Agreed	MD	SD	Total Disagreed	Total
1	Training should be given to both fresh and experienced people	12	30	42	84	15	1	16	100
2	In-house Training is more useful than sending employees to other organisation	16	33	35	84	13	3	16	100
3	Retaining the employees for longer duration brings success to the organisation rather than turning them out periodically	16	28	41	85	13	2	15	100

Source : Primary Data

respondents, irrespective of the reference group, moderately agreed (35%), agreed (33%), and strongly agreed (16%). There were also some opposing responses: Moderately disagreed (13%), strongly disagreed (3%). The overall impression of the respondents could be that In-house training was more useful for the employees than sending them to the other organisations for training.

In response to the statement "Retaining the employees for longer duration brings success to the organisation rather than turning them out periodically:" 41% of the respondents moderately agreed, 28% just agreed and 16% strongly agreed, totally 85% of the respondents agreed with the statement and 15% were in disagreement. Therefore retention of employees for a longer period in the organisation was reportedly giving success to the organisations, which ensures continuity in the activities both in quality and quantity.

With regard to the statement "Capacity Building for our staff is done in: " 41% of the respondents said that their staff were capacitated in field level activities and 40% of the respondents said they would train their staff in management aspects and 19% of them said that training would be given in administrative matters. Majority of them ie: 93 out of 225 respondents felt that capacity building of the staff should be one in field level activities.

As one of the management concepts, SWOT Analysis is done for any kind of activity in an organization for self assessment of the progress. When the respondents were probed whether SWOT Analysis was periodically done in their respective organizations 82% of them said "Yes", with 18% saying "No".

About 85% of the respondents have agreed with the statements mentioned on Training and Development aspects in the organizations.

Leadership, Monitoring and Evaluation (Reference Group-wise)

Providing good leadership, periodic monitoring and evaluation are a part of good Human Resource Management in an organization. These aspects were also examined by the researcher on the basis of reference group(Tribals, Dalits, Women, Children, Rural People, Youth and others) and the perceptions of the respondents were detailed below. (For Details see Table 3.16)

With regard to the statement "For the success of the organisation, Leader alone is responsible:" 37% of the respondents agreed, followed by 30% moderately agreed and 20% strongly agreed, totalling 87% of the respondents in agreement with the statement and 13% in disagreement of the statement. It indicated that leadership of the organisation played a major role in the success of the organisation.

When the managements of the Civil Society Organisations were probed whether employee should be continuously monitored and a day to day basis with the statement "Employees should be continuously monitored rather than assigning tasks and allowing them to complete the tasks" 48% moderately agreed, 17% just agreed and 12% strongly agreed. On the disagreement side of the statement 19% moderately disagreed and 4% strongly disagreed. The over all perception was 77% agreed and 23% disagreed. It showed that the managements felt that employees need to monitored and evaluated on a continuous basis without leaving them to complete the tasks on their own by fixing their own timelines.

For the statement "Leader should always guide and advise rather than involve in all day to day affairs", when we examine the perceptions of the respondents 42% were in agreement moderately, 31% just agreed, 11% strongly agreed, which indicated that the leader should always operate in a broader

Table 3.16: Responses of Managements of CSOs on Leadership, Monitoring& Evaluation of Employees (Reference group-wise)

(In percentage)

S.No	*Disagreed*	*Statement Total*	*SA*	*A*	*MA*	*Total Agreed*	*MD*	*SD*	*Total*
1	For the success of the organisation, Leader alone is responsible	20	37	30	87	9	4	13	100
2	Employees should be continuously monitored rather than assigning tasks and allowing them to complete the task	12	17	48	77	19	4	23	100
3	Leader should always guide and advise rather than involve in all day to day affairs	11	31	42]	84	13.5	2.5	16	100

Source : Primary Data

framework and guide and advise rather than involving in day to day affairs. It was felt that day to day governing matters relating to the organisation should be delegated and decentralised.

When it was examined how periodically the progress of staff was monitored in the respective organisations with the statement "In our organisation we monitor the progress of staff", 19% of the respondents said they would monitor annually, 38% said half-yearly, 27% said quarterly, 12% said monthly and 4% said fortnightly. When we take the over all perception, about 84% of the respondents said they would review the progress quarterly and above.

In response to the statement "Have you ever done cost effectiveness analysis of the activities" about 73% of the respondents said they would do cost effectiveness analysis of the activities. It could be seen that majority of the respondents were cost conscious and try to do activities in a cost effective manner.

With regard to the statements on Leadership, Monitoring and Evaluation of employees in the respective organizations, the respondents were in agreement to the degree of more than 77%.

Organisational Communication (Reference Group-wise)

Communication within the organization and among the employees was one of the aspects which was examined by the researcher based on the reference group (Tribals, Dalits, Women, Children, Rural People, Youth and others).

When it was examined whether downward and upward communication channels were encouraged in the respective organizations with the statement "We encourage both downward and upward communication channels", 81% of the respondents said they would. It could be attributed to the fact that the size of the CSOs was small and manageable and hence communication channels could be encouraged both ways.

In response to the statement "Employees should be encouraged to have inter-personal communications / relations while working in an organisation" a total of about 89.5% of the respondents were in agreement with the statement and 10.5% were in disagreement. To be elaborate, 38% of the respondents just agreed, 31.5% moderately agreed and 20% strongly agreed.

To sum up, it indicated that majority of the respondents were in favour of encouraging interpersonal communications/ relations in their respective organisations.

4

Case Study of Deccan Development Society (DDS)

The Charter of DDS

Deccan Development Society started as the commitment of a group of professionals to the people of its present project region (Zaheerabad), to continue a rural development project, which was abandoned by an industrial house due to its own politico-economic compulsions. The earliest objectives were to combine ecological and employment parameters to regenerate the livelihoods of the people in the area. It was also transfer of people-oriented technology. Gradually it has evolved into a programme which has three guiding principles: gender justice, environmental-soundness and people's knowledge. In recent years the issue of autonomy and control of local communities over their natural resources, agriculture, seeds, health, market and media have also taken the centre stage.

DDS is working for the past 15 years with Sanghams (village level groups) of poor women most of who are dalits. The society has a vision of consolidating these village groups into strong and vibrant organs of primary civil society and federate them into a strong pressure lobby for women, poor and dalits. A host of continuing dialogues, debates, educational and training programmes facilitated by the Society with the people tries to translate this vision into a reality.

Alongside this ideological role, the Society is trying to reverse the historical process of degradation of the environment and people's livelihood system in this region through a string of land-related activities like permaculture, community grain fund, community green fund, community gene fund and collective cultivation through land lease. Initiatives like sangam market are intended to play a proactive role and balance the exploitative nature of free market. These activities, alongside taking on the role of earthcare is also resulting in human care by giving the women a new-found dignity and profile in their village communities. Continuing from this strong base, the women are raising the issue of autonomy and control over their agriculture, seeds, farms and forests as well as market and media through developing a series of grassroots models like the Community Grain Fund, Community Gene Fund Community Green Fund and Community Media Trust. All these field experiences weave a strong matrix of sustainable rural development.

Organisation's Mission

The mission of the Society is to address and reverse the historical process of degradation of the environment and people's livelihood system in this region through a string of land-related activities like *Community Grain Fund, Community Gene Fund, Community Green Fund* and establishment of collective cultivation systems. The Society strives to help the local communities in general and dalit women in particualr to regain its autonomy over their natural resources, agriculture, genetic wealth, health, market and media

Strategic Objectives

DDS has developed a strong perspective on dalit and gender based development especially in the areas of food and nutritional security, community and women's control over genetic resources, ecological basis for food production, sustainable livelihood systems. In an increasing hostile political atmosphere where globalisation, privitisation, structural adjustment and conforming to the dictates of

Transnational corporations it is becoming very crucial to widen the sphere of debate and struggle for space for local communities in general and women and dalits in general.

The networking which DDS has initiated with different partners is trying to move forward this agenda on behalf of dalits and women particularly in the area of food sovereignty, genetic control and local knowledge systems.

Achievements of the Organization

- The perspectives of dalit women, espeically on food security and control over genetic resources, which DDS has been able to articulate in the national and international fora has received wide attention by developmental institutions, both governmental and non governmental
- The organisations seminal work on Alternative Public Distribution System and Community Gene Fund has been taken note by the highest policy making bodies in the country.
- The Society has been central for the contribution of the agrobiodiversity policy of the National Biodiversity Strategy and Action Plan, which is the Government of India's biodiversity policy as a commitment to the Convention on Biological Diversity [CBD]
- DDS is the only organisation in India which has set up a string of closely related community systems which are completely women controlled and managed. These include

  1. Community Grain Fund
  2. Community Gene Fund
  3. Community_Gene Fund
  4. Community Medicinal Commons
  5. Community Health

6. Community Media
7. Community Market

Through all these systems it has ensured that the critical control over the Community resources and knowledge lies with women.

Target Group(s): Organisation's (DDS) Main Beneficiaries (e.g. grass-root organisations, NGOs, women's organisations, individuals, others)

- DDS works with nearly 5000 women members in 75 villages belonging to *sanghams,* village level voluntary associations of women. Each *sangham* consists of 30 to 90 members, a majority of who are dalits.
- The partners for every programme taken up by the Society are identified by the members of the *sanghams*.
- DDS also works with coalition partners who share the ideals of ecological agriculture, gender justice, equity, participation and respect for traditional knowledge.

Organisation's Main Sectors of Intervention

i) Sustainable Agriculture
ii) Food and nutritional security
iii) Sustainable local livelihood systems
iv) Farmer lead science and research
v) Participatory development
vi) Community Control over natural resources
vii) Women centred local health systems
viii) Community controlled market
ix) Community conrolled women's media
x) Ecological education for rural children
xi) Legal and moral support for vulnerable single women

Organisation's Main Geographical Area(s)—Regions of Intervention

i) Primarily working in four mandals in Medak District of Andhra Pradesh in South India..

ii) Through the AP coalition in Defence of Diversity, working in all the 23 Districts of Andhra Pradesh

iii) As partner of SANFEC working in South Asia.

Finances (Income and Assets)

Total annual budget:	Current year(2006-07)	:	2,50,00,000.00
	Last year (2005-06)	:	2,53,00,000.00

Number and Qualification of Staff Working in the Accounting Section

1. 6 Commerce graduates working in Project Office and Hyderabad.
2. Two Senior retired persons from the Finance Department and Accounts wing of the Govt. Of India are working as Finance Manager and Dy. Finance Manager

Organisational Capacity

Administrative Staff

Number of full-time staff : Male: 25 Female: 17

Total number of administrative staff : 42

Programme/Project Staff (operational)

Number of full-time staff	:	Male: 29 Female: 36
Number of part-time staff	:	Male: 48 Female: 230
Total number of programme/ project staff	:	343

Overall Staffing

Number of permanent staff	:	Male: 54 Female: 53
Number of time-bound staff	:	Male: 48 Female: 230
Total number of staff	:	385
Remuneration		
Average monthly salary	:	Male:1,13,363 Female: 73,305
Board	:	Male:15,000 Female: 5,000
Management staff	:	Male:29,500 Female: 8,800
Programme staff	:	Male:47,141 Female: 32,332
Administrative staff	:	Male:36,722 Female: 22,113

Staff are provided 12% Provident Fund, Gratuity, HRA and Housing loans. The staff are covered under LIC of India for employees gratuity. The staff have been covered accident insurance policy.

Organisation's Policy for the Promotion of Women

DDS is an organisation with a total focus on empowerment of women. Therefore all its programmes are designed and managed by women. However due to historical reasons, we still have not been able to achieve complete parity in terms of the strength and remuneration. However at every point of time, with all things being equal, women get preference in appointment and promotion.

Training of Staff

Since much of the DDS work is based on learning from people, the staff are prepared for this work through processes of sensitisation and taking them through participatory tools and techniques.

Besides this, many members of the staff are given opportunities to attend appropriate training workshops offered by other institutions.

The DDS staff meetings and Karyakarta meetings normally get converted into training sessions for sensitising and analysing the contemporary issues that are relevant to the context of the Society's work.

Planning - Monitoring - Evaluation (PME)

- All programmes go through a continuous monitoring and evaluation system.
- At the primary level, each sangham in its weekly meeting discusses its own programmes and reviews its progress. This is done on a regular basis. One member of the DDS staff attends these meetings on a regular basis and makes her/his own notes on the progress/problems of the sangham and reports it back to the senior staff through a monthly written report.
- Each activity of the sangham is implemented by a separate committee. For eg if a sangham has a land lease programme, it will be implemented by a Land Lease Committee. If it has a watershed programme, a Watershed Committee implements the programme. These committees are composed of women from the sangham itself and elected by sangham members. The work of the committee is monitored and discussed in the sangham meetings.
- The Sangham leaders meet once every month and together report the progress of their own sangham progress. The collective of the sangham leaders provide their advise if something is going wrong.
- The Policy Group [Alternative Board] and the members of the DDS staff take part in these meetings to apprise themselves of the various stages of the

sangham activities. They also offer their suggestions and advise.

- Programmes planning and implementation is discussed in detail in the monthly staff meetings.
- The policy group discusses the major points with the staff every month in the monthly staff meeting
- Periodic internal evaluation is done by a Core Monitoring Team consisting of the Project Director, Joint Directors, Programme Coordinators.
- Major activities and performances are presented to the Board of Directors who provide their advise and suggestions.

Use of External Expertise for Training

External expertise has been utilized in the following areas. Providing trainings for PRA methods.

- Training on watershed management programme
- Training in raising plant nurseries and grafting them
- Forestry programmes
- Permaculture techniques and methods
- Gender workshops
- Trainings in Alternative Educational methods to Night School teachers, Pacha Saale Teachers and Balwadi Teachers
- Awareness about GM Crops, WTO, TRIPS.

Participation of Target Groups in the PME Process

- Target groups are involved at every stage: at the stage of designing, implementation, monitoring and evaluation as described above.
- In recent years, every group, through a three-tier PRA system has also designed its own budget

Programme/ Project Setup

a) whether log frame based or not

The Log frames are not a regular part of the DDS programmes and projects except for one or two projects, where LFs have become an integral part. DDS believes in an organic development of its projects since it is basically participatory and community-led and therefore the initiatives cannot be straitjacketed within the logic of log frames.

b) Monitoring and indicators

All the activities of the project are community based with the interventions planned and implemented through the women associations. The monitoring of the activities as per the plans will take place at different levels. Village level Women associations meet weekly to monitor the progress of the activities. Groups of women members also form committees and meet regularly to share information and cross monitor their activities.

Monitoring at the organisational level takes place monthly by a group of senior level management staff and the person in-charge of the activities The field staff with the leaders of individual women association monitor and review the progress of the project during monthly staff meetings. Any problems that have arisen are discussed and solutions proposed.

Accountability

a) Main decision making mechanisms and planning processes

Over the last five years, a significant attempt has been made by DDS to decentralise the decision making and administration of funds at the sangham level. Each DDS sangham has its own bank account in the following areas:

- Community Grain Fund
- Community Green Fund

- Community Gene Fund
- Medicinal Commons
- Dalit Watersheds

Besides, about thirty sanghams have their own bank accounts to cover their own credit and savings.

All these are operated by them independently through a committee of elected members. All operational decisions are taken by the members of sanghams themselves.

The sanghams regularly network between themselves to provide a continuous horizontal sharing of experiences. These experience sharing sessions devote themselves alternately to discuss the philosophy and ideologies of DDS, the way they are being implemented by each sangham and the issues related to the monetary transactions between sanghams. This arrangement has not only passed on a significant amount of financial decision making to the junior field level staff but also has created an environment of constant reality check vis a vis the larger ideals of the Society and its translation into field level activities.

b) Main beneficiaries of the activities of DDS

Mainly women who come from the marginalised sections of society. They are primarily composed of Dalits and include the vulnerable and the poor from other communities also. Since women take the lead in all the initiatives they are the primary beneficiaries.

c) Beneficiary involvement in planning, implementation and monitoring of the activities.

In almost all of its activities, the community partners, both in terms of individuals and groups, are consulted right from the beginning. A series of continuing dialogues with the women leaders of the DDS sanghams creates the idea for a particular intervention. This idea leads to a number of participatory decision making processes, at the village sangham level, among the karyakartas and the staff council.

Finally a cumulation of these participatory exercises the decision making. The primacy of the decision making rests with the village sanghams and is later fine tuned by the other actors. The implementation is entirely done by the sanghams with a bit of guidance by the staff members.

The monitoring is a collaborative activity. The primary monitoring is done by the committees of women in the village sanghams who are engaged in a particular activity. This is co monitored by the staff members who are concerned with those particular sanghams. The staff of the DDS have formed their own monitoring committee which has representatives from different sectors of DDS activities. Finally the Monitoring committee reports to the Staff Council.

At the Sangham level, the implementation and monitoring is done 100% by women. The staff members consist of both women and men almost in equal numbers. The Staff monitoring Committee is also made up of women and men in equal numbers.

DDS' interaction with beneficiaries/ other stakeholders

Every week the sanghams hold their own meetings in their villages which is attended by a member of the DDS staff who takes notes from the meetings. Every month the leaders of the sanghams, all of who are women come together for a meeting at different DDS centres. This meeting is invariably attended by all the staff concerned with those areas. This is the direct interaction that happens on a regular basis.

Besides these, there are periodic meetings held of the different committees of DDS which compose entirely of the beneficiaries. They include the various activity related committees such as PDS committee, Seed Committee, Land Lease Committee, Balwadi Committee etc. There are also meetings which are not particularly related to an activity. They include the Legal Committee, Policy Group etc. In all these meetings the staff directly interact with the communities.

d) Expected number of beneficiaries of DDS activities (direct and indirect)

The DDS directly serves about 5000 women. Indirectly it impacts nearly 500,000 persons. Of this approximately 40% would be women, though this figure is not computed exactly.

Gender

a) DDS's policies with regard to women's empowerment and gender equality within the programme activities and within the organisation. DDS is an organistion completely dedicated to enabling women to regain their control over natural resources, agriculture, health, market and media. Therefore it is totally addressed to help women regain their status in the agrarian society.

Though there may be more men on the so called management positions because of historical reasons such as their seniority in the organisation, in practice, all decisions in DDS are taken collectively by the Staff Council in which women outnumber men and therefore play a major role.

Two major bodies like Monitoring Committee and Facilitation Committee which help the Staff Council make decisions have men and women in equal numbers.

Many bodies like the Community Media Trust, Market Committee etc which make major decisions are all women groups. Similarly in most of the project activity committees women occupy 90% of the positions.

The POLICY GROUP, also described as Alternative Board of Directors, which guides DDS staff in all decisions is fully composed of rural dalit women.

b) Contacts of DDS with women's organisations (at local, national or international level)

DDS is one of the first promoters and members of **Women's Networks** in AP. Though it is not a formal member of any women's organisations, it regularly and actively responds to the invitations to participate and/or co-organise events with NAWO, National Commission for Women such other organisations at the national level. In the area of gendered agriculture and food security, DDS is the leading organisation both within India and internationally. DDS has participated in Beijing Conference for women and World March of Women to prevent violence against women.

c) Internal gender expertise in DDS

At the grassroots level, the women of DDS have gone through a number of gender workshops and therefore have acquired a certain level of consciousness on gender issues. The organisation also has a gender coordinator at the medium-management level.

At the Board level, DDS has four very noted gender activists. Dr Rukmini Rao, Dr Shanta Sinha, Ms Jamuna and Ms Akhileswari. The last mentioned is the key promoter of Indian Association of Women Journalists.

Information Communication Technologies (ICTs)

DDS is working with the women in a series of local autonomies that include:

- Food Sovereignty [Autonomy over food production]
- Seed Sovereignty [Autonomy over seeds: local production, local storage]
- Autonomy over natural resources.

It is in this context that the ICT work of DDS is situated. The autonomies over food and seed, in the context of a globalising world, we think needs to be supported by an autonomous market and an autonomous media that can be controlled by the local communities, particularly the women.

This thinking has produced a Community Media Trust set up by the DDS, but completely autonomously owned and operated by the women of the area. Ten trustees operate the Trust, all of who are local women belonging to dalit castes.

The Community Media Trust has two wings:

- Video Production Centre
- Community FM Radio Station.

The Video Production Centre is operated by about eight women half of who are non literate.They are not only engaged in their own video productions but also train other women in their own area as well as farmers in the South Asia region.

The Video production unit regularly produces programmes that further the ideologies of the women of DDS sanghams. They also contribute occassionally to the mainstream television channels in the area both for newscasts as well as stand alone programmes.

Rallies and Workshops

DDS has lead a number of major campaigns:

- Campaign against genetically modified crops
- Campaign against transnational occupation of Indian Agriculture
- Campaign against Vision 2020 policy of A.P. Government, which, if implemented, will further marginalise and decimate the small and the marginal farmers, and compel them to surrender to new colonial institutions of contract and corporate farming.
- Farmers Juries on the issues of corporate agriculture. Celebrations of major events like World Environment Day, International Womens day and World Food Day.
- Workshops on Genetically modified crops, biotechnology
- Campaign for relevant education for rural children
- Campaign on participatory decision making process
- Campaign against family violence
- Campaign against child labour.

Networking

- The Society has also been championing the cause of ecological and agro-biodiversity with local, regional, national and international communities. It has founded the Andhra Pradesh Coalition in Defence of Diversity, a coalition of over 142 civil society organisations from all the 22 districts of Andhra Pradesh.
- DDS is also networking with a number of national NGOs on this issue besides being a leading member of the SANFEC (South Asian Network for Food, Ecology and Culture), a coalition of over 200 ecological groups from Bangladesh, Nepal, India, Pakistan and Sri Lanka.

Publications

- Agro-biodiversity in Andhra Pradesh, a Farmer's Perspective Uncultivated Foods and the Poor
- Genetic engineering, Agriculture and Food
- Crops of Truth
- Mana Varu-Mana Vantalu - an introduction to traditional cuisines of Medak District, Andhra Pradesh.
- Paata Pantala Parichayam - an introduction to the traditional crops of Medak District, Andhra Pradesh
- Prajateerpu; A citizen jury /Scenario workshop on Food and Farming Fu-tures for Andhra Pradesh, India
- Vermicomposting
- Organic composting
- Sustainable Development
- Contract Farming at Kuppam
- Strategy and Action Plan for Agro Biodiversity for Sub-state site in the Deccan, Andhra Pradesh, an

outcome of the MOBILE BIODIVERSITY FESTIVAL of the Deccan Development Society.

Responses of Employees on HR and Change Management Practices in DDS

To further explore the Change Management aspects in the management as well as with the employees, a survey was conducted, in which, Out of 383 employees on the payrolls of DDS under different categories, 100 employees were taken on stratified random sampling basis and the questionnaire was administered to take their opinion on Human Resource Management and Change Management Aspects in their Organisation.

Age Group

Out of 100 employees taken for the sample ,27% are in the age group of 20-30 years, 29% are in 30-40 years age group, 27% are in 40-50 age group and17% are in more than 50 years age group.

Number Years of Experience

In DDS, 30% of the sample employess have less than 5 years of experience, 27% with 5-10 years of experience, 28% with 10-15 years of experience and 15% are with more than 15 years of experience. Broadly, 57% of them are having less than 10 years of experience, whereas 43% of the employees have more than 10 years of experience.

Experience in the Present Organisation

As regards the experience of sample employees in DDS 38% of them have put in 1-4 years of experience, followed by 26% of them with 5-8 years of experience, 22% of them with 9-12 years and 14% of them have more than 12 years of experience. Broadly 64 % of them have been serving DDS for less than 8 years and 36% of them are with more than 8 years experience.

Educational Qualifications

When the educational Qualification of the employees was examined 14% of the sample were below Graduates, 37% of them were Graduates, 28% possessed Post Graduate qualification and 21% of them had Professional Degrees.

Marital Status

Of the sample employees taken for the study, 76% of them were married, whereas 24% of them were Unmarried.

Area of Specialisation

When we examined the area of specialization in which the employees were working, it was found that 6% of them were involved in Administrative tasks,52% of them were involved in field activities, 5% of them in Financial Management, 26% of them in Capacity building Activities and finally 11% of them were involved in Policy Advocacy. When the fact that most of the Capacity Building activities take place in the field is taken into consideration almost 78% of the employees were involved in the field related activities, whereas only 22% of them handle Administrative, Financial Management and Policy Advocacy related tasks.

When asked whether DDS was the first civil society organization they were working with, only 46% said, 'Yes' and 54% said 'No'. Therefore for majority of them DDS was not the first CSO to work with.

Familiarity with DDS

When it was enquired with the sample employees of DDS whether they knew anything about DDS before joining it, 62% of the employees said' Yes', whereas 38% said 'No', which indicated that majority of them were familiar with DDS even before becoming an employee of that organization.

Recruitment into the Organisation

When it was asked how the employees were recruited into

DDS, 13% of the sample employees said that they were recruited through News Paper Advertisement, 38% through reference, 5% through Manpower Consultancies, 21 of them responded by saying that they approached the management directly and finally, 23% of them replied that they were spotted by the management while working with other organizations and were invited to join DDS. The trend shows that DDS is mostly relying on recruitment through reference as well as through direct spotting and inviting to join DDS.

Factors for Joining DDS

It is known that many factors like Need for job, interest in Social Service, persuasion from a friend and getting motivated by the work DDS is doing etc; prompts employees to join an Organisation. When the question was put to the sample employees as to what prompted them to join a job with DDS, 50% of them said Need for Job prompted them to join, followed by 25% who said that they joined out of interest in Social Service, 10% said they joined out of Persuasion from a friend already worked in DDS and 15% said they were motivated by the work DDS was doing and that prompted them join in the Organisation. There could be many guiding factors to work in any Organisation, nevertheless, need for job is the one that prompts majority of the employees to work in an organization.

Expectations from the Organisation

When the employees were asked as to what was the most important thing they look for from the Organisation, 32% said that they would look for commitment and sincerity of the management, 20% of them said they would look for salaries and benefits, 39% of them said they would look for service rendered to the poor, a 9% said they would look for functional freedom. Since civil Society Organisations are service Organisations, it is but natural that the employees also need to be service oriented and they look for similar service-mindedness from management too.

Shift in Focus Area during the Last 5-10 Years

When it was questioned whether the employees observed any shift in focus area during the last 5-10 years, 63% said 'Yes', while 37% said ' No'. By focus area it is meant, the core area of activity the organisation is involved in.

Employee Motivation

As a part of Human Resourse Management in DDS, motivation of the employees was examined through various statements aimed at obtaining their perceptions on the HR management. (For details see Table 4.1)

When we examined the perceptions of the respondents on the statement "Service motto of the organisation motivates me to work in this organisation", 43% strongly agreed,36% just agreed, 14% moderately agreed. Over all range of agreement was about 93%.

With respect to the statement "The organisation should expand the activities to various Geographical locations in the State/Country:", about 87% of the respondents had reportedly agreed that their organization should expand activities to other geographical locations, which gave them motivation through the feeling that their organization was big. When the range of agreement was looked into, 37% strongly agreed, 33% just agreed, 17% moderately agreed.

When we examined the motivation of employees to work for monetary benefits with the statement "Monetary benefits alone motivate me to work in this organisation:", the degree of agreement was 77% and degree of disagreement was 23%. When we looked into details 38% just agreed, followed by 20% moderately agreed, 19% strongly agreed. There were also respondents who moderately disagreed (13%) and strongly disagreed(10%). It indicated that money alone was not the motivating factor for employees to work in DDS.

With regard to the statement "Job satisfaction is important for me:", almost all the employees felt (93%) that job

Table 4.1: Monitoring & Evaluation Details showing the responses of employees of DDS on motivation

(In Percentage)

S.No	Statement	SA	A	MA	Total Agreed	MD	SD	Total Disagreed	Total
1	Service motto of the organisation motivates me to work in this organisation:	43	36	14	93	3	4	7	100
2	The organisation should expand the activities to various Geographical locations in the State/ Country:	37	33	17	87	7	6	13	100
3	Monetary benefits alone motivate me to work in this organisation:	19	38	20	77	13	10	23	100
4	Job satisfaction is important for me :	39	30	24	93	5	2	7	100
5	Strong and committed leadership motivates employees in the organisation:	17	42	27	86	10	4	14	100

Source : Primary Data

satisfaction was of utmost importance to them with degrees of agreement varying from 39% strongly agreed, 30% just agreed and 24% moderately agreed.

The researcher attempted to examine how leadership motivated the employees in DDS with the statement "Strong and committed leadership motivates employees in the organisation:", The degree of agreement varied from just agreed (42%), moderately agreed (27%) and strongly agreed (17%). A total of about 86% of the respondents were in agreement with the statement where as 14% of the respondents were in disagreement, indicating that strong and committed leadership did not motivate some of the employees of the organization.

The analysis indicated that the Motivational levels were relatively higher, as majority of the respondents were in agreement with the statement.

Recruitment and Training

The recruitment and training is one of the components of Human Resource Management of an organization and as apart of the research we examined the perceptions of employees of DDS on recruitment and training in their organization and the details are as follows. (For details see Table 4.2)

When the researcher enquired with the respondents whether competency alone should be used as a recruitment criteria using the statement "Employees should be recruited based on competency alone:", the respondents were overwhelmingly in agreement (91%). The degree of agreement varied from 44% moderately agreed, followed by 28% just agreed and 19% strongly agreed. Though there were respondents who were in disagreement, but degree varied from moderately disagreed (7%), strongly disagreed (only 2%).

With regard to the statement "Educational qualification alone is sufficient for better performance in a CSO:", 78% of

Table 4.2 : Responses of Employees of DDS on Recruitment and Training in their Organization

(In Percentage)

S.No	Statement	SA	A	MA	Total Agreed	MD	SD	Total Disagreed	Total
1	Employees should be recruited based on competency alone:	19	28	44	91	7	2	9	100
2	Educational qualification alone is sufficient for better performance in a CSO:	4	47	27	78	7	15	22	100
3	Training in motivation is essential for every employee:	18	40	22	80	18	2	20	100
4	For improving the performance on the job, training is compulsory:	14	32	34	80	10	10	20	100
5	My organisation trains me periodically in attitudinal change:	8	18	27	53	28	19	47	100

Source : Primary Data

the respondents agreed and 22% disagreed. When we look into details the degree of agreement varied from just agreed (47%), moderately agreed (27%), strongly agreed (4%) and degree of disagreement varied from moderately disagreed (15%) and strongly disagreed (7%), which indicated that a few respondents felt that for better performance in CSOs educational qualification alone would not be sufficient.

When the researcher examined whether employees should be trained in motivation with the help of the statement "Training in motivation is essential for every employee:" about 40% of the respondents just agreed, followed by 22% moderately agreed and 18% strongly agreed which total to about 80% of the respondents in agreement.

With respect to the statement "For improving the performance on the job, training is compulsory:", the respondents were reportedly having divided opinions with 80% of them in agreement and 20% of them in disagreement. Going by the majority perceptions of the respondents, training seemed to be compulsory for improving the performance on the job.

When we examined whether DDS trained its employees in attitudinal change on a periodic basis through the statement "My organisation trains me periodically in attitudinal change", the respondents were almost equally divided between agreement with the statement (53%) and disagreement with the statement (47%).

The over all impression of the respondents was on the positive side indicating that recruitment process was suitable to them. There was an exception to the statement "On Training in attitudinal change", on which the respondents were almost equally divided between 'Yes' and 'No'.

Change Management

The employees of DDS were examined through the following statements on Change Management that was happening in their organization and their perceptions were obtained as followed: (For details see Table 4.3)

The preparedness of the employees of the organization to take up any task given by the management at any time was examined with the statement "I am ready to take up the task/ assignment given to me by my management immediately :" A total of about 86% of the respondents were prepared to take up the assignment at any time, whereas only 14% of the respondents were in disagreement. The degree of agreement varied from just agreed (38%), followed by strongly agreed (31%) and moderately agreed (17%).

With respect to the statement "My organisation's goals/ objectives are changing according to the situation", the perceptions of the respondents varied from moderately agreed (34%), followed by just agreed (32%), strongly agreed (17%) amounting to 83% of agreement which showed that majority of the respondents were aware that their organization(DDS) had been changing the goals and objectives according to the situation.

When it was enquired with the respondents whether they were willing to improve their performance by observing change agents, with the help of the statement "I learn to increase my performance by observing others (change Agents):", about 89% of the respondents were in agreement and 11% were in disagreement. The disagreement among the respondents for the statement could be due to the possibility that they could not identify proper change agents in their organizations or that they were not willing to follow others to improve their performance.

In response to the statement " Are there any such change agents from whom you can learn in your organisation:", about 80% of the respondents with varied degrees of agreement like 32% strongly agreed,23% just agreed and 25% moderately agreed, were able to identify change agents or trend setters in their organization from whom they could learn. The fact that 20% of them were not in agreement with the statement indicated that they could not identify any change agents.

Table 4.3: Responses of Employees of DDS on Change Management in their Organisation

(In Percentage)

S.No	*Statement*	*SA*	*A*	*MA*	*Total Agreed*	*MD*	*SD*	*Total Disagreed*	*Total*
1	I am ready to take up the task/assignment given to me by my management immediately :	31	38	17	86	7	7	14	100
2	My organisation's goals/objectives are changing according to the situation	17	32	34	83	9	8	17	100
3	I learn to increase my performance by observing others (change Agents):	21	42	26	89	8	3	11	100
4	Are there any such change agents from whom you can learn in your organisation:	32	23	25	80	14	6	20	.100
5	Founder's background like age, Education, domicile, experience and affiliation are important for the success of the organisation	19	38	24	81	14	5	19	100
6	The organisation is surviving because it takes its employees into confidence in decision making		36	21	26	83	9	8	17 100

Source : Primary Data

For the statement "Founder's background like age, Education, domicile, experience and affiliation are important for the success of the organization", the respondents reportedly had strongly agreed (19%), moderately agreed (24%) and just agreed (38%) with over all agreement among 81% of the respondents. The fact that 19% of the respondents were in disagreement to the statement indicated that a few people in the organization were not keen on founder's background for the success of the organization.

When response to the statement "The organisation is surviving because it takes its employees into confidence in decision making:" a total of 83% of the respondents felt that they were involved in participatory decision making in the organization. The degree of agreement ranged from strongly agreed (36%), moderately agreed (26%), just agreed (21%). There were also some respondents who were in disagreement (17%) with the statement.

On almost all the statements on which the respondents were obtained, the employees were in agreement indicating that Change Management had been happening in DDS.

Human Capital Management

For any organization Human Capital has become one of the important assets. Unless the human capital is properly managed the organization can not be run successfully. Some aspects relating to Human Capital Management have been examined and following are the details. (For details see Table 4.4)

In response to the statement "Management of resources is the root cause for the success of organization", about 89% of the respondents were in agreement and 11% of the respondents were in disagreement. If we look into the details 47% just agreed, 27% moderately agreed and 18% strongly agreed, which was an indication that efficient resource management would lead to the success of the organization.

Table 4.4 : Responses of Employees of DDS on Human Capital Management in their Organization

(In Percentage)

S.No	*Statement*	*SA*	*A*	*MA*	*Total Agreed*	*MD*	*SD*	*Total Disagreed*	*Total*
1	Management of resources is the root cause for the success of organisation	18	47	24	89	7	4	11	100
2	Human Capital is more important than Social and Financial Capital for the success of the organisation	7	25	26	58	24	18	42	100
3	Delegation and Decentralisation is essential for the success of any organisation	19	43	25	87	9	4	13	100

Source: Primary Data

When the question of importance of Human Capital was asked through the statement "Human Capital is more important than Social and Financial Capital for the success of the organization", 58% of the respondents felt that human capital was more important than social and financial capital, whereas 42% of the respondents felt other wise.

With regard to the statement "Delegation and Decentralisation is essential for the success of any organization", a total of about 87% of the respondents were in agreement and 13% in disagreement. If we look into the details, 43% of the respondents just agreed, 25% moderately agreed and 19% strongly agreed, which indicated that in stead of centralization employees were looking for delegation and decentralization.

When the researcher attempted to obtain the opinion of the respondents on the area in which they would like to initiate changes in their organization, if changes had to be made,34% of the respondents replied that they would initiate changes in performance measurement and review, followed by 22% who said that reporting system would be changed, 15% said working style, 15% said procedures and 14% said training and development.

When the respondents were asked if they wanted to work in DDS even if there were changes in policy, leadership and management style, 68% said "Yes", which indicated that majority of the employees would like to continue in the organization.

Except on the statement on importance of " Human Capital over Social and Financial capital", the respondents were overwhelmingly in agreement.

Tools of Change Management

For coping with changing situation and growing demands from managements the employees of DDS were asked to give preferences on the areas, in which they would like to be trained or the areas, in which the management should conduct training programmes for the employees of the organization on a 1-5 point scale. These areas of training where the respondents wanted to be trained were termed as Tools of Change Management. The details of the preferences, individual tool wise, are as followed. The weightage given to the preferences were; maximum for 1 and minimum for 5. (For details see Table 4.5)

With regard to "Organisation Management" as a tool of Change Management, 53% of the total respondents gave first preference, followed by 13% of the respondents giving 2nd preference, 13% giving 3rd preference, 15% giving 4th preference and 6% giving 5th preference.

In response to "Role and Goal clarity", as a tool of Change Management, 39% of the respondents gave 2nd preference, followed by 27% of the respondents giving 1st preference.

In response to "Reporting Relationship", 37% of the respondents gave 2nd preference, followed by 27% giving 5th preference and 21% of the respondents gave 3rd preference.

Regarding "Motivation" as a tool of Change Management, only 4% of them gave 1st preference, followed by 31% giving 2nd preference. But 41% of the respondents gave the 5th preference for the tool, if they wanted to be trained in.

In response to "Leadership Activities", as a tool of Change Management, 45% desired for getting trained as a 1st preference, followed by 24% as 2nd preference.

With respect to "Communication Skills", as a tool of Change Management, majority of them(33%) preferred on 2nd priority, followed by 29% of the respondents preferring 3rd priority.

When enquired with the respondents about " Inter Personal Relations", as a tool of Change Management, 36% gave 4th preference followed by 29% giving 2nd preference.

When the respondents were asked to rate "Group Dynamics", as a tool of Change Management, 44% of them opted for 2nd preference, followed by 22% opting 5th preference.

Table 4.5: Responses of Employees of DDS on "Tools of Change Management" in their Organisation

(In Percentage)

S.No	Tools of Change Mgmt	Order of Preference					Total
		1	2	3	4	5	
1	Organisation Management	53	13	13	15	6	100
2	Role and goal clarity	27	39	15	14	5	100
3	Reporting relationships	9	37	21	6	27	100
4	Motivation	4	31	17	7	41	100
5	Leadership activities	45	24	17	9	5	100
6	Communication skills	21	33	29	7	10	100
7	Inter personal relations	8	29	24	36	3	100
8	Group Dynamics	17	44	7	10	22	100
9	Conflict Management	24	29	7	8	32	100
10	Stress Management	21	14	19	16	30	100
11	Personality Development	11	34	14	36	5	100
12	Facilitation Skills	40	27	14	14	5	100
13	Systems thinking and understanding	16	29	16	32	7	100
14	Problem solving skills	13	27	33	16	11	100
15	Knowledge of interventions	39	19	22	10	10	100
16	Advocacy / Buy-in skills	18	32	23	18	9	100
17	Negotiation / contracting skills	25	21	14	32	8	100
18	Coping skills	24	19	10	5	42	100

Source: Primary Data

In response to training in "Conflict Management", as a tool of Change Management, 24% of the respondents gave 1st preference, followed by 29% giving 2nd preference and 32% giving 5th preference.

When the respondents were asked to give their order of preference for " Stress Management", as a tool of Change Management, 30% of them gave 5th preference, followed by 21% of them giving 1st preference and 19% giving 3rd preference.

In response to the Change Management tool of " Personality Development", 36% of the respondents put it as 4th preference, followed by 34% as the 2nd preference. Only 11% had chosen it as the 1st preference.

When it was enquired with the respondents on the preference given by them for training on "Facilitation Skills", as a Change Management tool, 40% of them chose it as the 1st preference followed by 27% as the 2nd preference.

With regard to "Systems thinking and understanding", as a Change Management tool, 32% of the sample employees of DDS reportedly preferred as their 4th choice, followed by 29% as the 2nd choice and only 16% preferred as 1st choice.

With respect to "Problem Solving Skills", as a Change Management tool, about 33% of the respondents gave 3rd preference, followed by 27% as 2nd preference and 16% as 4th preference.

In response to "Knowledge of Interventions", as a Change Management tool, 39% preferred as the 1st choice, followed by 22% as 3rd choice and 19% as 2nd choice, which indicated that employees want to know what kind of interventions were being taken up in the organization.

With regard to " Advocacy/ Buy-In Skills", as a Change Management tool, 32% of the respondents gave it 2nd preference, followed by 23% giving it 3rd preference and 18% of the respondents giving it 1st preference.

When the respondents were asked to give their preferences on "Negotiation/ Contracting Skills", as a Change Management tool, 25% of them gave 1st preference, 32% gave 4th preference and 21% gave 2nd preference.

In response to "Coping Skills", as a Change Management tool, 42% of the respondents gave it 5th preference, followed by 24% giving it 1st preference and 19% giving it 2nd preference. It could be seen that majority of the respondents were reportedly not keen on getting trained in "Coping Skills".

The overall preference of the respondents on the area in which they would like to be trained in could be prioritized as Organization Management, Facilitation Skills, Leadership Activities, Knowledge of Interventions followed by Group Dynamics, Role and Goal clarity, Reposting relationships and Personality Development. It could be seen that the respondents were choosing non-traditional areas for training, which indicated that they wanted to gear themselves for the new challenges of future.

5

Case Study of MV Foundation

The M.Venkatarangaiya Foundation, a registered Trust, was established in 1981 in memory of educationist and historian Prof. Mamidipudi Venkatarangaiya. It began as a research institution on issues relating to social transformation. Today, the Foundation is building the capacities of the community in rural areas for abolition of child labour by popularising school education. It also works towards empowering women through collective action on issues relating to livelihoods and natural resource management.

Basic Principles of Organization and Decision-making Processes

1. All members of the foundation firmly believe in the charter of basic principles of emancipation of child rights. (The non-negotiables)
2. Given this framework the staff has autonomy in decision making and working out the details of the programme. The staff at the local level share full responsibility for planning, implementation and monitoring of the programme. The decisions thus taken are respected and even encouraged.
3. The innovative initiatives that emerge from such a process are shared with all the other members in MVF. It is in learning from these experiences; understanding the significance of such an exercise, and conceptualizing the key elements in the strategy

adopted that a policy is evolved to be replicated on a large scale.

4. The development of the programmes of MVF, and the lessons learnt become a part of the collective experience of the MVF as a whole. In this sense the MVF's programme develops in a spiral fashion from one stage to the next. The entire process does not repeat from the start when it begins in a new area but takes off where the MVF is at the moment.
5. The MVF has always worked with the village community. Every occasion is utilised to see that the community leadership is in the forefront giving strength to the programme. This also results in the community owning up the programme. In other words the MVF avoids substituting for the community. Thus the MVF is not a direct implementing agency but acts as a facilitator of the programme.
6. All efforts of mobilization results, in establishing forums, committees, and pressure groups, leading to institution building with a process for a systematic review of the programme.
7. Through this process of MVF's constant interaction with the institutions thus established new agendas for action emerge. It gains confidence to take up challenging tasks.
8. Simultaneously the staff of the MVF also graduates to take on new assignments and roles in the organization. Their capacities are thus enhanced.
9. Involvement of the staff in conducting surveys, analysis of data, self-evaluation studies and reports become essential components in drawing up a plan of action and also in responding to the demands.

Strategy

The strategy adopted is essentially based on age and

gender. Older children (9-14 years) are put through a bridge course, which equips them to catch up with regular school--going children. Younger children are directly admitted to schools. There is a detailed follow-up programme, which ensures a minimum dropout rate, and makes the education system more accessible to working children. Very often, this involves addressing issues such as getting birth certificates, negotiating with teachers for admission, ensuring hostel admissions, and so on. Education activists under the programme are trained to identify and resolve every possible impediment in the way of converting a child labourer into a full-time student.

Donors and Partners

MVF's programme has been supported by the Government of India, SERP DPIP Govt. of Andhra Pradesh, UNDP/ NORAD, UNICEF, IPEC-ILO, HIVOS, Catholic Relief Services, JRD Tata Trust, Sir Dorabji Tata Trust, and HYDERABAD ROUND TABLE - 8 among others.

MVF partners with parents and children, elected representatives, employers and officials. In this context the BKVV, a teachers' forum against child labour with over 1500 members is unique in that it defines for the first time, the role of a teacher in the context of child labour. The first generation learners as education activists have infused the programme with a sense of urgency and idealism, contributing significantly to its success.

MVF as an Implementing Agency in Andhra Pradesh

Based on the non-negotiable principle that 'no child works and every child attends full time formal school as a matter of right', MVF has been working towards abolition of child labour in all its forms and mainstreaming them into formal schools, for over a decade now. It began its work from 3 villages in 1991. Gradually it expanded, to cover 6000 villages in 158 mandals of Ranga Reddy, Srikakulam, Vizianagaram,

Adilabad, Mahbubnagar, Chittoor, Nalgonda, Kurnool, Kadapa, East Godavari, Visakapatnam, Anantapur, Warangal districts of Andhra Pradesh. Cumulatively, over a period of 15 years about 3,90,000 children have thus been withdrawn from work and sent to schools in these 13 districts of Andhra Pradesh. Of these 50,000 children have been mainstreamed through the bridge course camps to formal schools, government social welfare hostels and residential schools. During this period it monitored the status of 1,000,000 children in and out of school. The organization profile and Staff profile of MVF are very judiciously organized for successful implementation of their programmes.

Currently it monitors the status of over 400,000 children in 6 districts of Andhra Pradesh namely Ranga Reddy, Nalgonda, Warangal, Hyderabad, Adilabad and Kurnool.

MVF conducts mobilisation drives through its large band of committed youth volunteers who relentlessly pursue every child and plan for getting him/her into school. This includes handling such sensitive issues as age at marriage for girls.

In the course of implementing its programme MV Foundation has built alliances with the following:

- MVF has founded an alliance of school teachers in the State for liberation of child labour viz. Bala Karmika Vimochana Vedika with over 2500 school teachers in 18 Districts of Andhra Pradesh.
- Works in alliance with 30,000 local youth volunteers, in Andhra Pradesh who have participated in rallies, marches, public meetings at the village, mandal and district level in campaign against child labour.
- Networks with over 1500 Panchyat Raj RIs in all the Districts of MVF project area.
- Partnership with women's groups, School Education Committees for campaign and mobilisation. Formation of federations of these groups at the Mandal and

District levels, on the issue of child labour.

- Child Rights Protection Forums (CRPFs) in every village and also at the Mandal and the District levels with a membership of 20000.

MVF has worked in tribal and forest regions, coastal belts, deserts, and dry land farms among fishermen, nomads, tribals, landless poor agricultural labourers and quarry workers who have all responded to the programme.

MVF does not set up parallel institutions to the schools, social welfare hostels, gram Panchayats and other state institutions. Thus over a period of time the MVF program has blended with the existing government programs enriching rather than supplanting them. Significant policy changes have been made all over the state of Andhra Pradesh as a result of MVF's work.

- The Andhra Pradesh government has changed its policy to define child labour as all children out of school and announced that the only place a child must be is in school.
- Conventional non-formal education programmes in the state have changed into day schools.
- Bridge Course camps have become a central element in getting children into school and are being replicated in other areas.

MVF strongly believes that to be replicable it must work through existing institutions and build community pressure/ support to strengthen these institutions and their capacities to ensure that they commit themselves to protection of child rights and education.

Further MVF believes that much of its replicability arises out of the clear set of principles 'the non-negotiables' that it has evolved and it is this that holds the key to the program replicability.

The Non Negotiables

1) All children must attend full-time, formal day schools
2) Any child out of school is a child labourer
3) All labour is hazardous and harms the overall growth and development of the child
4) There must be total abolition of child labour and
5) Any justification perpetuating the existence of child labour must be condemned.

M.V. Foundation as a Technical Support and National Resource—Other States

MVF is also operational in five other states of India viz., Assam, Bihar, Madhya Pradesh, Tamil Nadu, and Maharashtra apart from the neighbouring country of Nepal.

Assam

The M.V.Foundation started working in 9 blocks in 9 districts of Assam in 2002 by providing technical support to the Sarva Siksha Abhiyan of the Government of Assam. The resource persons helped in setting up bridge course camps in each of these blocks. Children were identified and mobilized for the residential bridge course camps, teachers were trained and systems such as review for teachers and children, meetings with parents, involving the local community in the running of the bridge course camps were introduced.

Madhya Pradesh

From June 2004 onwards, M.V.Foundation is providing support to the Rajya Siksha Mission in 25 blocks in 25 districts of Madhya Pradesh. 29 resource persons have been deputed for this purpose. During this reporting period MVF conducted intensive training and mobilisation activities in the state.

Trainings were conducted for BRCs, CAC, Sarpanches and PTAs from 39 districts during the first week of January 2005. Exposure visits were conducted as part of the training programme. The importance of community mobilisation, before setting up of RBCs and NRBCs was explained to them.

During this period, Other NGOs also sought MVF support in the implementation of their programme. Action Aid was given support in eight districts where its partners are implementing programmes. Orientation programmes were conducted to NGOs like Jana Sahas Samsthan, Bachpan and Samavesh. Volunteers and staff of the same NGOs were also taken on an exposure visit to MVF's programme in Andhra Pradesh.

Maharashtra

Apeksha Homeo Society

Two resource persons from the M.V.Foundation are working with an NGO, Apeksha Homeo Society, in Maharashtra since July 2004. The NGO works in 5 blocks in Amaravati and Akola districts. In Amaravati, the concentration is in the tribal area, Melghat. They requested for support from the M.V.Foundation for community mobilization and formation of Child Rights Protection Forums.

Montfortian Child Rights Movement

In collaboration with the Montfortian Child Rights Movement in Ballarshah, Chandrapur District, Maharashtra two volunteers from MVF built capacities of the staff and members of gram panchayats in 19 gram panchayats. The work involved conducting of youth meetings and rallies, training programmes and exposure visits to Adilabad, involvement of officials of the labour and education departments in the campaign, survey of children in schools and out of schools and conducting an enrollment drive.

Tamil Nadu

Kancheepuram Block

Five resource persons are working in one block, covering 43 panchayats, in the Kancheepuram District in Tamil Nadu providing support to a local NGO called Hand in Hand since June 2004. It was seen that the NGO was running evening schools and a parallel centre for tribal children. Meetings were held with parents and these children were all mobilized for the local school. It was then decided with the NGO staff that these centres can be run as motivation centres but they could not become an alternative for schools.

Nagapattinam District

Following the Tsunami on 26th December 2004 Action Aid International invited M. V. Foundation to help out with an assessment of the situation in respect of the Children's' education in the Tsunami affected areas in Tamilnadu. The objective of the project is to focus on the universalisation of education, covering all the children in these villages, to ensure that at the end of the project period, processes are built to ensure that every child is in school.

Bihar

Action Aid (partner NGOs)

MVF extended its technical support to Bihar on invitation from Action Aid in the year 2005. Currently it is extending the support to the NGOs in Samastipur block of Bihar.

Nepal

Save the Children (Japan), Partner NGO

M V Foundation deputed one of its senior resource person to assist Shreepurraj Community Development Centre (SCDC), an NGO in Nepal. It is working in four Village Development Committees (VDCs) of Saptari district on the issue of child rights. Each VDC covers 2-3 schools. SCDC covered 4 VDCs comprising 10 villages with 10 schools.

Advocacy

M.V. Foundation networked with national advocacy groups such as CACL, CRWSF, HAQ, IACR, and facilitated a campaign to bring about an amendment to the Child Labour (P&R) Act 1986. Over 845 NGO's in 14 States participated and 100,000 post cards were sent to 700 M.P's on the issue following which a PIL was filed in the Supreme Court decision of which is still pending. This has received wide media publicity.

Cotton Seeds Issue

Hundreds of thousands of children work in production of hybrid cottonseeds in India. They toil relentlessly day after day in horrendous conditions on the farms working long hours in the sun, exposed to harmful pesticides. M.V.Foundation (MVF) worked with seed organizers in Kurnool and Mahaboobnagar Districts, had discussions with the MNCs on ways to collaborate to eliminate child labour on cottonseed farms. MVF was successful in passing the message to the farmers and seed organisers that they cannot continue with the practice of employing children in cotton farms as " they are constantly under watch'.

Child Rights Protection Forums (CRPF)

In the process of the mobilizing communities to establish a social norm that no child must work and every child must attend full time formal school, the M.V.Foundation enlisted the support from every section of society. When there was a specific case of protecting a girl child from marriage or of withdrawing a bonded labour child from bondage, supporters of child rights in villages formed themselves into a Child Rights Protection Forum. In the beginning these forums were adhoc and got organized to sort out a specific case of violation of children's rights. As they became active they felt the need to get institutionalized into formal forums to protect children's rights.

With the setting up of the Forums every section in the village is thus alerted that violating the rights of the child would not be tolerated. The Forums help in the community internalising the idea that children need to go to schools.

Some Activities taken up by the CRPF are:

- Solved hundreds of problems that children faced during admissions into schools such paying school fees, school uniforms, transfer certificates, caste certificates and so on.
- Whenever any instance of corporal punishment came to their notice it was taken up with higher authorities to see that action was taken against such teachers.
- Mobilised support from the entire village to stop child marriages.
- Took up incidents of gross violation of child rights such as employment of children in factories under exploitative working conditions, death of children due to pesticide inhalation with the government, the media and also the National Human Rights Commission
- They heard the appeals of children wanting to abandon work in favour of joining schools and took up problems faced by them either in school or at home.

Campaign against Child Marriages

It was found that a major reason for parents getting their daughters married off at an early age was their anxiety towards the security of the girl, the issue of ensuring safety for girls in the villages and creating a supportive environment for them was also taken up with the community. A signature campaign was held in the villages in Andhra Pradesh with certain specific demands in relation to the Child Marriage Restraint Bill, 2004. Young girls, school teachers, gram panchayat members, mandal Parishad members, child rights activists, youth, women and parents actively participated in this campaign. Significantly, the State Human Rights Commission issued notices to the government to arrest all child marriages and report on action taken.

Note on Training Conducted by M.V. Foundation

M.V. Foundation (MVF) has been organizing training programmes for its own staff and all the stakeholders involved in mobilizing community, for withdrawal of children from work and mainstreaming them into formal schools. Sessions on the following non-negotiables, principles for emancipation of child labour have been indispensable for conducting trainings.

1. All children must attend full-time formal day schools.
2. Any child out of school is a child labourer.
3. All work/labour is hazardous, and harms the overall growth and development of the child.
4. There must be total abolition of child labour.
5. Any justification perpetuating the existence of child labour must be condemned.

During the first phase of work the emphasis of all trainings has been to build an atmosphere to enable children to abandon work. It focuses on all components of social mobilization. The following is the list of trainings for the staff of M.V. Foundation.

Participants	*No. of days*	*Contents of training.*
1.Youth	5 days – 1 day in each spell over a period of 6 months.	• Survey details. • Need for survey • utilizing survey • for campaign and identification of local potential partners in the village. • On non-negotiable principles.
2.Volunteers	3 days	• On components of social mobilization. • Role of local institutions- VEC, Gram Panchayats. • Role of Volunteers. • Girl Child and Education. • Reading books, articles related to child labour and education. • FAQs on child labour and education.
3.Educationactivists.	7 days	• On components of social mobilization. • Role of local institutions- VEC, Gram Panchayats. • Role of Volunteers. • Girl Child and Education. • Reading books, articles related to child labour and education. • FAQs on child labour and education. • Classroom practices, pedagogy for older children.
4. Organisers	9 days in 3 spells of 3 days each during the	• Team building and leadership qualiies • Basic principles of organization and management of the programme.

	course of one year.	• Basic principles of implementation of the programme and expansion to new village areas. • Acts • Teachers Forums. • Recognition of Parents demand for education- discussion.Role of MVF vis-a-vis community and the government.
5. Mandal In- charges.	7 days	• Training conducted by specialists with focus on team building, qualities of leadership, delegation of responsibility, modalities to receive feed back, entrusting new responsibilities and identification of strengths and weaknesses of the team.
6.DistrictIncharges	7 days	Training conducted by specialists with focus on team building, qualities of leadership, delegation of responsibility, modalities to receive feedback, entrusting new responsibilities and identification of strengths and weaknesses of the team.
7. Volunteers for Long Term Bridge Course Camps	35 days – 5 spells during the course of the year	• Subject wise training in planning to teach older children. • Preparation for public examination. • Setting up a library • Book reading. • Preparation of children for Formal Schools..
8. Short Term Bridge Course Camps	21 days in 3 spells	• Bridge course objectives. • Counselling children and preparing them for studentship. • Teaching them the alphabet, ability to read and write. • Teaching basic Mathematics.

The content of trainings for youth and volunteers is designed based on their experience in the programme. In addition to the above, MVF staff undergo constant on job training through review meetings and exposure visits... Senior staff of MVF have also undergone structured training programmes of three days each in two spells on issues relating to the following issues:

- Debates on Poverty and Development,
- Role of State and Public Action;
- Social Transformation in India
- Organisation and Development
- Education and Development.

The resource persons for such trainings have been from universities and reputed NGOs.

MVF as a Training Agency

M V Foundation has never hesitated to respond to requests from either NGOs or elected representatives of the government. As such, it has conducted workshops, trainings, orientation programmes for several national and international agencies.

- MVF has conducted training sessions/programs for hundreds of NGOs on the issue of child rights in Andhra Pradesh and elsewhere in the country.
- It has also oriented government schoolteachers in Andhra Pradesh in the past five years. All district level officials of Departments of Education, Social Welfare, Women and Child Welfare Govt. of Andhra Pradesh have been given orientation and an exposure to MVF's project area.
- Trainings for State level staff of DPEP from all the states in the country.

- Perspective-building workshops on 'Child Labour and Education' for NGOs in the country supported by UNDP.
- Capacity Building workshops, on the job training, planning and monitoring for other NGOs and the DPEP/SSA in other states such as Assam, Madhya Pradesh, Orissa, Rajasthan, West Bengal, Maharashtra, and Tamil Nadu have been conducted sponsored by GOI, Indus Project (ILO), Sarva Siksha Abhiyan, NCERT, Labour department)
- Capacity Building workshop for PRIs, Youth groups, school committees and staff of Aasman Nepal (NGO) for Save the Children Fund–Japan.

Responses of Employees on HR and Change Management Practices in MVF

A total work force of 1328 have been working either on salary basis or voluntary basis in MV Foundation. Among them Day school activities (416), Organisations (426) and Teaching staff (106) contribute their services on voluntary basis and for a little amount of honorarium. A summary was conducted for the rest of 380 employees on the regular payrolls of MVF under different categories, 100 employees were taken on stratified random sampling basis and the questionnaire was administered to take their opinion on Human Resource Management and Change Management Aspects in their Organisation.

Age Group

Out of 100 employees taken for the sample, 18% are in the age group of 20-30 years, 39% are in 30-40 years age group, 34% are in 40-50 age group and 9% are in more than 50 years age group.

Number Years of Experience

In MVF, 19% of the sample employess have less than 5

years of experience, 37% with 5-10 years of experience, 36% with 10-15 years of experience and 8% are with more than 15 years of experience. Broadly, 56% of them are having less than 10 years of experience, whereas 44% of the employees have more than 10 years of experience.

Experience in the Present Organisation

As regards the experience of sample employees in MVF 33% of them have put in 1-4 years of experience, followed by 23% of them with 5-8 years of experience,29% of them with 9-12 years and 15% of them have more than 12 years of experience. Broadly 56 % of them have been serving MVF for less than 8 years and 44% of them are with more than 8 years experience.

Educational Qualifications

When the educational Qualification of the employees was examined 14% of the sample were below Graduates, 46% of them were Graduates, 23% possessed Post Graduate qualification and 17% of them had Professional Degrees.

Marital Status

Of the sample employees taken for the study, 83% of them were married, whereas 17% of them were Unmarried.

Area of Specialisation

When we examined the area of specialization in which the employees were working, it was found that 6% of them were involved in Administrative tasks, 45% of them were involved in Field Activities, 9% of them in Financial Management, 30% of them in Capacity building Activities and finally 10% of them were involved in Policy Advocacy. When the fact that most of the Capacity Building activities take place in the field is taken into consideration almost 75% of the employees were involved in the Field related activities, whereas only 25% of them handle Administrative, Financial Management and Policy Advocacy related tasks.

When asked whether MVF was the first civil society organization they were working with, only 53% said, 'Yes' and 47% said 'No'. Therefore for majority of them MVF was not the first CSO to work with.

Familiarity with MVF

When it was enquired with the sample employees of MVF whether they knew anything about MVF before joining it, 67% of the employees said' Yes', whereas 33% said 'No', which indicated that majority of them were familiar with MVF even before becoming an employee of that organization.

Recruitment into the Organisation

When it was asked how the employees were recruited into MVF, 10% of the sample employees said that they were recruited through News Paper Advertisement, 33% through reference, 5% through Manpower Consultancies, 32% of them responded by saying that they approached the management directly and finally, 20% of them replied that they were spotted by the management while working with other organizations and were invited to join MVF. The trend shows that MVF is mostly relying on recruitment through reference as well as through direct spotting and inviting to join MVF.

Factors for Joining MVF

It is known that many factors like need for job, interest in Social Service, persuasion from a friend and getting motivated by the work MVF is doing etc; prompts employees to join the Organisation. When the question was put to the sample employees as to what prompted them to join a job with MVF, 19% of them said Need for Job prompted them to join, followed by 42% who said that they joined out of interest in Social Service, 13% said they joined out of Persuasion from a friend already working in MVF and 26% said they were motivated by the work MVF was doing and that prompted them join in the Organisation.

Expectations from the Organization

When the employees were asked as to what was the most important thing they look for from the Organisation, 38% said that they would look for commitment and sincerity of the management, 24% of them said they would look for salaries and benefits, 29% of them said they would look for service rendered to the poor, a 9% said they would look for functional freedom. Since civil Society Organisations are service Organisations, it is but natural that the employees also need to be service oriented and they look for similar service-mindedness from management too.

Shift in Focus Area during the Last 5-10 Years

When it was questioned whether the employees observed any shift in focus area during the last 5-10 years, 63% said 'Yes', while 37% said ' No'. By focus area it is meant, the core area of activity the organisation is involved in.

Employee Motivation

As a part of Human Resource Management in MVF, motivation of the employees was examined through various statements aimed at obtaining their perceptions on the HR management. (For details see Table 5.1)

When we examined the perceptions of the respondents on the statement "Service motto of the organisation motivates me to work in this organisation:" , 30% strongly agreed, 40% just agreed, 23% moderately agreed. Over all range of agreement was about 93%.

With respect to the statement "The organisation should expand the activities to various geographical locations in the State/Country:", about 94% of the respondents had reportedly agreed that their organization should expand activities to other geographical locations, which gave them motivation through the feeling that their organization was big. When the range of agreement was looked into, 24% strongly agreed, 47% just agreed, 23% moderately agreed.

Table 5.1: Responses of Employees of MVF on Motivation

(In percentage)

S.No	*Statement*	*SA*	*A*	*MA*	*Total Agreed*	*MD*	*SD*	*Total Disagreed*	*Total*
1	Service motto of the organisation motivates me to work in this organisation:	30	40	23	93	5	2	7	100
2	The organisation should expand the activities to various Geographical locations in the State/Country:	24	47	23	94	6	0	6	100
3	Monetary benefits alone motivate me to work in this organisation:	16	39	35	90	5	5	10	100
4	Job satisfaction is important for me :	31	34	31	96	3	1	4	100
5	Strong and committed leadership motivates employees in the organisation:	20	34	37	91	6	3	9	100

Source : Primary data

When we examined the motivation of employees to work for monetary benefits with the statement "Monetary benefits alone motivate me to work in this organisation:", the degree of agreement was 90% and degree of disagreement was 10%. When we looked into details 39% just agreed, followed by 35% moderately agreed, 16% strongly agreed. There were also respondents who moderately disagreed (5%) and strongly disagreed(5%). It indicated that money alone was not the motivating factor for employees to work in MVF.

With regard to the statement "Job satisfaction is important for me:", almost all the employees felt (96%) that job satisfaction was of utmost importance to them with degrees of agreement varying from 31% strongly agreed, 34% just agreed and 31% moderately agreed.

The researcher attempted to examine how leadership motivated the employees in MVF with the statement "Strong and committed leadership motivates employees in the organisation:", The degree of agreement varied from just agreed(34%), moderately agreed(37%) and strongly agreed(20%). A total of about 91% of the respondents were in agreement with the statement where as 9% of the respondents were in disagreement, indicating that strong and committed leadership did not motivate some of the employees of the organization.

The Motivation of the employees was overwhelmingly in agreement with all the statements, indicating that the leadership could motivate the employees well.

Recruitment and Training

The recruitment and training is one of the components of Human Resource Management of an organization and as apart of the research we examined the perceptions of employees of MVF on recruitment and training in their organization and the details are as follows.(For details see Table 5.2).

Table 5.2: Responses of Employees of MVF on Recruitment and Training in their Organisation

(In percentage)

S.No	Statement	SA	A	MA	Total Agreed	MD	SD	Total Disagreed	Total
1	Employees should be recruited based on competency alone:	15	35	36	86	12	2	14	100
2	Educational qualification alone is sufficient for better performance in a CSO:	11	38	40	89	8	3	11	100
3	Training in motivation is essential for every employee:	12	34	37	83	14	3	17	100
4	For improving the performance on the job, training is compulsory:	18	32	35	85	12	3	15	100
5	My organisation trains me periodically in attitudinal change:	8	37	39	84	13	3	16	100

Source : Primary data

When the researcher enquired with the respondents whether competency alone should be used as a recruitment criteria using the statement "Employees should be recruited based on competency alone:", the respondents were overwhelmingly in agreement (86%). The degree of agreement varied from 36% moderately agreed , followed by 35% just agreed and 15% strongly agreed. Though there were respondents who were in disagreement, but degree varied from moderately disagreed (12%), strongly disagreed (2%).

With regard to the statement "Educational qualification alone is sufficient for better performance in a CSO:", 89% of the respondents agreed and 11% disagreed. When we look into details the degree of agreement varied from just agreed (38%), moderately agreed (40%), strongly agreed (11%) and degree of disagreement varied from moderately disagreed (8%) and strongly disagreed (3%), which indicated that a few respondents felt that for better performance in CSOs educational qualification alone would not be sufficient.

when the researcher examined whether employees should be trained in motivation with the help of the statement "Training in motivation is essential for every employee:" about 34% of the respondents just agreed, followed by 37% moderately agreed and 12% strongly agreed which total to about 83% of the respondents in agreement.

With respect to the statement "For improving the performance on the job, training is compulsory:", the respondents were reportedly having divided opinions with 85% of them in agreement and 15% of them in disagreement. Going by the majority perceptions of the respondents, training seemed to be compulsory for improving the performance on the job.

When we examined whether MVF trained its employees in attitudinal change on a periodic basis through the statement "My organisation trains me periodically in attitudinal change", the respondents were divided between agreement with the statement (84%) and disagreement with the statement (16%), leaving the impression that periodic training had been taking place in attitudinal change for the employees.

Despite some respondents on the disagreement with regard to the statements, the overall trend was in agreement to the statements.

Change Management

The employees of MVF were examined through the following statements on Change Management that was taking place in their organization and their perceptions were obtained as followed .(For details see Table 5.3)

The preparedness of the employees of the organization to take up any task given by the management at any time was examined with the statement "I am ready to take up the task/ assignment given to me by my management immediately :" A total of about 91% of the respondents were prepared to take up the assignment at any time, whereas only 9% of the respondents were in disagreement. The degree of agreement varied from just agreed (41%), followed by strongly agreed (25%) and moderately agreed (25%).

With respect to the statement "My organisation's goals/ objectives are changing according to the situation", the perceptions of the respondents varied from moderately agreed (43%), followed by just agreed (26%), strongly agreed (14%) amounting to 83% of agreement which showed that majority of the respondents were aware that their organization (MVF) had been changing the goals and objectives according to the situation.

When it was enquired with the respondents whether they were willing to improve their performance by observing change agents, with the help of the statement "I learn to increase my performance by observing others (change Agents):", about 87% of the respondents were in agreement and 13% were in disagreement. The disagreement among the respondents for the statement could be due to the possibility that they could

Table 5.3: Responses of Employees of MVF on Change Management in their Organization

(In percentage)

S.No	Statement	SA	A	MA	Total Agreed	MD	SD	Total Disagreed	Total
1	I am ready to take up the task/ assignment given to me by my management immediately :	25	41	25	91	5	4	9	100
2	My organisation's goals/objectives are changing according to the situation	14	26	43	83	11	6	17	100
3	I learn to increase my performance by observing others (change Agents)	11	38	38	87	9	4	13	100
4	Are there any such change agents from whom you can learn in your organisation	11	25	42	78	21	1	22	.100
5	Founder's background like age, Education, domicile, experience and affiliation are important for the success of the organisation	9	43	35	87	11	2	13	100
6	The organisation surviving because it takes its employees into confidence in decision-making	12	33	39	84	12	4	16	100

Source: Primary data

not identify proper change agents in their organizations or that they were not willing to follow others to improve their performance.

In response to the statement " Are there any such change agents from whom you can learn in your organisation:", about 78% of the respondents with varied degrees of agreement like 11% strongly agreed,25% just agreed and 42% moderately agreed, were able to identify change agents or trend setters in their organization from whom they could learn. The fact that 22% of them were not in agreement with the statement indicated that they could not identify any change agents.

For the statement "Founder's background like age, Education, domicile, experience and affiliation are important for the success of the organization", the respondents reportedly had strongly agreed (9%), moderately agreed (35%) and just agreed(43%) with over all agreement among 87% of the respondents. The fact that 13% of the respondents were in disagreement to the statement indicated that a few people in the organization were not keen on founder's background for the success of the organization.

When response to the statement "The organisation is surviving because it takes its employees into confidence in decision making:" a total of 84% of the respondents felt that they were involved in participatory decision making in the organization. The degree of agreement ranged from strongly agreed(12%), moderately agreed(39%), just agreed(33%). There were also some respondents who were in disagreement (16%) with the statement.

The over all impression of the respondents was in favour of the statements except in the case of the statement on " Any change agents from whomyou can learn from your organization", where the percentage of disagreement was about 22%.

Human Capital Management

For any organization Human Capital has become one of the important assets. Unless the human capital is properly managed the organization can not be run successfully. Some aspects relating to Human Capital Management have been examined and following are the details. (For details see Table Number 5.4)

In response to the statement "Management of resources is the root cause for the success of organization", about 84% of the respondents were in agreement and 16% of the respondents were in disagreement. If we look into the details 41% just agreed, 30% moderately agreed and 13% strongly agreed, which was an indication that efficient resource management would lead to the success of the organization.

When the question of importance of Human Capital was asked through the statement "Human Capital is more important than Social and Financial Capital for the success of the organization", 87% of the respondents felt that human capital was more important than social and financial capital, whereas 13% of the respondents felt otherwise.

With regard to the statement "Delegation and Decentralisation is essential for the success of any organization", a total of about 95% of the respondents were in agreement and 5% in disagreement. If we look into the details, 36% of the respondents just agreed, 37% moderately agreed and 22% strongly agreed, which indicated that in stead of centralization employees were looking for delegation and decentralization.

When the researcher attempted to obtain the opinion of the respondents on the area in which they would like to initiate changes in their organization, if changes had to be made,32% of the respondents replied that they would initiate changes in performance measurement and review, followed by 11% who said that reporting system would be changed, 10% said working style, 14% said procedures and 33% said training and development.

Table 5.4: Responses of Employees of MVF on Human Capital Management in their Organization

(In percentage)

S.No	Statement	SA	A	MA	Total Agreed	MD	SD	Total Disagreed	Total
1	Management of resources is the root cause for the success of organisation	13	41	30	84	13	3	16	100
2	Human Capital is more important than Social and Financial Capital for the success of the organisation	14	36	37	87	11	2	13	100
3	Delegation and Decentralisation is essential for the success of any organisation:	22	36	37	95	3	2	5	100

Source : Primary data

When the respondents were asked if they wanted to work in MVF even if there were changes in policy, leadership and management style, 74% said "Yes", which indicated that majority of the employees would like to continue in the organization.

In almost all the statements pertaining to Human Capital Management aspects in the organization, all the respondents were in similar degrees of agreement giving an impression that MVF was following the same polices, which the employees had seen wishing for.

Tools of Change Management

For coping with changing situation and growing demands from managements the employees of MVF were asked to give preferences on the areas, in which they would like to be trained or the areas, in which the management should conduct training programmes for the employees of the organization on a 1-5 point scale. These areas of training where the respondents wanted to be trained were termed as Tools of Change Management. The details of the preferences, individual tool wise, are as followed. The weightage given to the preferences were; 1st preference given maximum of 5 points and 5th preference given minimum of one point. (For details see Table 5.5)

With regard to "Organisation Management" as a tool of Change Management, 28% of the total respondents gave first preference, followed by 12% of the respondents giving 2nd preference, 24% giving 3rd preference, 29% giving 4th preference and 7% giving 5th preference.

In response to "Role and Goal clarity", as a tool of Change Management, 29% of the respondents gave 2nd preference, followed by 20% of the respondents giving 1st preference.

In response to " Reporting Relationship", 38% of the respondents gave 2nd preference, followed by 25% giving 5th preference and 8% of the respondents gave 3rd preference.

Table 5.5: Responses of Employees of MVF on Tools of Change Management in their Organization

(In percentage)

S.No	*Tools Of Change Mgmt*	*Order of Preference*					*Total*
		1	*2*	*3*	*4*	*5*	
1	Organisation Management	28	12	24	29	7	100
2	Role and goal clarity	20	29	30	18	3	100
3	Reporting relationships	17	38	8	12	25	100
4	Motivation	35	32	24	5	4	100
5	Leadership activities	33	32	21	8	6	100
6	Communication skills	45	8	12	30	5	100
7	Inter personal relations	30	10	18	10	32	100
8	Group Dynamics	31	3	15	12	39	100
9	Conflict Management	29	33	20	12	6	100
10	Stress Management	20	34	9	13	24	100
11	Personality Development	26	19	15	35	5	100
12	Facilitation Skills	12	8	29	21	30	100

13	Systems thinking and understanding	28	10	14	32	16	100
14	Problem solving skills	10	16	28	17	29	100
15	Knowledge of interventions	16	17	24	32	11	100
16	Advocacy / Buy-in skills	9	24	11	17	39	100
17	Negotiation / contracting skills	21	6	12	30	31	100
18	Coping skills	12	18	31	21	18	100

Source : Primary data

Regarding "Motivation" as a tool of Change Management, only 35% of them gave 1st preference, followed by 32% giving 2nd preference. But 4% of the respondents gave the 5th preference for the tool, if they wanted to be trained in.

In response to "Leadership Activities", as a tool of Change Management, 33% desired for getting trained as a 1st preference, followed by 32% as 2nd preference.

With respect to "Communication Skills", as a tool of Change Management, majority of them(45%) preferred on 1st priority, followed by 30% of the respondents preferring 4th priority.

When enquired with the respondents about " Inter Personal Relations", as a tool of Change Management, 32% gave 5th preference followed by 30% giving 1st preference.

When the respondents were asked to rate "Group Dynamics", as a tool of Change Management, 39% opting 5th preference, followed by 31% of them opted for 1st preference.

In response to training in "Conflict Management", as a tool of Change Management, 29% of the respondents gave 1st preference, followed by 33% giving 2nd preference and 20% giving 3rd preference.

When the respondents were asked to give their order of preference for " Stress Management", as a tool of Change Management, 34% of them gave 2nd preference, followed by 24% of them giving 5th preference and 20% giving 1st preference.

In response to the Change Management tool of "Personality Development", 35% of the respondents put it as 4th preference, followed by 26% as the 1st preference. Only 19% had chosen it as the 2nd preference.

When it was enquired with the respondents on the preference given by them for training on "Facilitation Skills", as a Change Management tool, 30% of them chose it as the 5th preference followed by 29% as the 3rd preference.

With regard to "Systems thinking and understanding", as a Change Management tool, 32% of the sample employees of MVF reportedly preferred as their 4th choice, followed by 28% as the 1st choice and only 16% preferred as 5th choice.

With respect to "Problem Solving Skills", as a Change Management tool, about 29% of the respondents gave 5th preference, followed by 28% as 3rd preference and 17% as 4th preference.

In response to "Knowledge of Interventions", as a Change Management tool, 32% preferred as the 4th choice, followed by 24% as 3rd choice and 17% as 2nd choice and 16% of 1st choice, which indicated that employees want to know what kind of interventions were being taken up in the organization.

With regard to " Advocacy/ Buy-In Skills", as a Change Management tool, 39% of the respondents gave it 5th preference, followed by 24% giving it 2nd preference and 17% of the respondents giving it 4th preference, but only 9% gave 1st preference.

When the respondents were asked to give their preferences on " Negotiation/ Contracting Skills", as a Change Management tool, 31% of them gave 5th preference, 30% gave 4th preference and 21% gave 1st preference.

In response to "Coping Skills", as a Change Management tool, 31% of the respondents gave it 3rd preference, followed by 21% giving it 4th preference and 18% giving it 5th preference. It could be seen that majority of the respondents were reportedly not keen on getting trained in "Coping Skills".

Among all the Change Management Tools for the respondents to choose from, the first preference as their top choice was given for Communication skills, Motivation, Leadership activities and Group Dynamics followed by Reporting Relationships, Conflict Management, Leadership activities and Motivation as the second preference. It indicate that the respondents were keen on traditional areas of training for them to face the challenges of future.

6

Findings, Conclusions and Recommendations

Findings from Cross Case Analysis of 2 Case Studies—DDS and MVF

After studying in depth about the two cases which were taken for the study, the researcher attempted to analyse the two cases across various parameters. Apart from the similarities on various aspects the researcher found the following differences between the two cases. ie., DDS and MVF.

Cross Analysis Based on Organization Management of DDS and MVF

With regard to the background of the founder, DDS founder had a background of social service and retired from service, whereas in the case of MVF, the founder was from educational background.

With regard to the reference group, DDS works for Dalits, Women, Children and Rural people, while MVF works only for the upliftment of the children.

When we compare the ideology of the organizations DDS claimed to have Gandhian Ideology, whereas MVF followed Gandhian as well as Marxian Ideology.

As regards the mission statement, both the organizations were reportedly having the mission statement.

With regard to the statements, “Every organization should have goals to function effectively”,”Every organization should have objectives to achieve the goals”, “Functioning of the organisation depends on the motto with which we are working”, “Have you changed the activities over the period since inception” and “Activities are mere activities. They should also be used as strategies to achieve the goals”, both the managements of DDS and MVF were reportedly in agreement completely.

With regard to the statement on “We are working strictly in line with the objectives set out at the time of Incorporation of the organization”, management of DDS strongly agreed, where as management of MVF moderately disagreed, which indicated that there was a shift in the objectives of MVF over the period.

When the researcher examine the perceptions of the management of DDS and MVF on the statement “Organisational success depends on adapting to new challenges every time instead of a Consistency approach”, DDS was in moderate disagreement, where as MVF management was in strong agreement with the statement indicating that there was a basic difference of opinion between the two organizations.

Internal Decision-making

With regard to the internal management or decision making process in the organizations in DDS all major decisions pertaining to the activities of the organization, core committees were reportedly taking them, where as in MVF centralized leader took decisions on activities like major focus shift, monitoring of activities, promotion of employees, pay hike/ incentives to employees and board of governors took decisions on financial decisions, employee recruitment and core committees decided on planning of activities, monitoring of activities and performance appraisals and ad-hoc committees were involved in decision making process regarding implementation process for the activities, staff monitoring and problem solving.

Recruitment

In response to the statement "Recruitment of employees in the organisation should be based on policies such as gender proportion, Caste proportion", management of DDS strongly agreed, where as management of MVF moderately disagreed.

In response to the statement "Employees should be recruited based on Competency alone", management of DDS just agreed, where as management of MVF moderately disagreed, which showed that there was a basic difference of opinion on the statement.

With respect to the procedure of recruiting the staff also DDS management felt that recruitment through advertisements and direct approach by the aspirants was better, where as MVF management said that they would prefer to recruit by spotting the prospective employees and inviting them to join the organization.

With regard to the statements "Qualified Specialist staff are helpful for the organization", "Capacity Building for our staff is done in", "We assess our Strengths, Weaknesses, Opportunities and Threats (SWOT) periodically", and the perceptions of the managements of both DDS and MVF were same.

With regard to the commitment of the staff to the cause, DDS management felt it moderate, where as MVF management felt it high.

Training and Development

With respect to the statements "Experienced Generalist staff are useful for the organization", "Retaining Employees in the organisation is becoming difficult", "We are remunerating the employees according to their Competency / Skills / Qualifications", "Training should be given to both fresh and experienced people', "In-house Training is more useful than sending employees to other organization", the difference in perception of the managements of DDS and MVF was varying between strongly agree and just agree to moderately disagreed and strongly disagreed. It could be analysed that the difference in perception was certainly there, but in a small degree.

Leadership and Motivation

With regard to the statement "For the success of the organisation, Leader alone is responsible", DDS management moderately disagreed, but MVF management strongly disagreed, indicating that success of the organization depended not on leader alone, but on the entire team.

In response to the statement "Employees should be continuously monitored rather than assigning tasks and allowing them to complete the task", both the managements were reportedly having opposing views to the extreme degrees, strongly agree and strongly disagree. They held differing opinions on the statements.

When the researcher explored the periodicity of monitoring the progress of the staff, DDS management was reportedly conducting progress monitoring on a quarterly basis, where as MVF management did the same on annual basis.

With regard to the statements "Have you ever done cost effectiveness analysis of the activities", "We encourage both downward and upward communication channels", "Employees should be encouraged to have inter personal Communications / relations while working in an organization", "Retaining the employees for longer duration brings success to the organisation rather than turning them out periodically", the managements of both DDS and MVF were reportedly having same perceptions.

In response to the statement "Leader should always guide and advise rather than involve in all day to day affairs", the researcher found very thin line of difference of perception, which was varying between just agreed for DDS and strongly agreed for MVF.

Both the managements of DDS and MVF were reportedly having strong belief in decentralized decision making process, which would strength the organization as well as the individual. They also were of the opinion that space should created for all levels to express their opinions and views. Both the managements felt that success of CSOs lied in empowering the employees to plan, execute and evaluate the work done by them.

Cross Analysis based on Employees Survey in DDS and MVF

In the vertical study conducted by the researcher on the employees of two CSOs namely DDS and MVF, the perceptions of the employees on the Human Resource Management practices and Change Management aspects were also in varying degrees of agreement and disagreement.

Cross Analysis of Personal Profiles

Apart from differences in the basic activities, in which both the organizations were involved in, there were also some similarities between them. With respect to the profile of age, majority of the employees of DDS(56%) were in the age group of 20-40 years, where as majority of the employees of MVF(57%) were in the age group of 20-40 years. But employees of more than 50 years of age were more(17%) in DDS and the employees of the same age group were relatively less(9%) in MVF.

When we compare number of years of experience of employees in both the organizations, 56% of the employees had experience of less than 10years and 44% of the employees had more than 10years in MVF. In DDS also 57% had less than 10yeras and 43% of the employees had more than 10 years experience.

The general responses of the employees regarding aspects like, experience in the present organization, Educational qualifications, marital status, area of specialization, familiarity with the organization they were working with, recruitment process in the organization, factors for joining respective organizations, the expectations of the employees from the organisations and on shift in focus areas during the last 5-10 years, were more or less similar with very little degree of variation. It could be seen from the analysis that employees of both the organizations felt similarly on most of the personal as well as organizational issues.

Employee Motivation

With regard to employee motivation in both the organizations, the responses of the employees to the statements "Service motto of the organisation motivates me to work in this organization", "The organisation should expand the activities to various Geographical locations in the State/ Country", "Monetary benefits alone motivate me to work in this organization", "Job satisfaction is important for me", "Strong and committed leadership motivates employees in the organization", were overwhelmingly in agreement with them. We could see the percentage of the employees, who were in disagreement with the statements was very negligible. This trend indicated that the employees were highly motivated to work in the respective organizations and their motivational objectives were completely in line with the objectives of the organization.

Recruitment and Training

In the area of Recruitment and Training in the respective organizations, the perception of the employees on the statements "Employees should be recruited based on competency alone", "Educational qualification alone is sufficient for better performance in a CSO", "Training in motivation is essential for every employee", "For improving the performance on the job, training is compulsory", was almost similar in DDS and MVF. The degree of agreement had been around 85% with the degree of disagreement being about 15%. It could be inferred that the employees in both the organizations were of the same opinions on the given statements. But in response to the statement "My organisation trains me periodically in attitudinal change", majority of employees of MVF(84%) opined that their organization trained them periodically on attitudinal change, where as the employees of DDS were almost divided in their perceptions with degree of agreement varying between 53% in agreement and 47% in disagreement. Out of this it could be inferred that almost half of the employees were not sure about conducting trainings for employees in attitudinal change periodically. The researcher could gauge from the respondents of DDS that they desired trainings to be conducted in attitudinal change .

Change Management

With regard to the statements on Change Management aspects, for which responses were obtained, the ultimate analysis of the perceptions of the employees indicated that in both DDS and MVF, they were of same opinion. In response to the statements "I am ready to take up the task/assignment given to me by my management immediately", "My organisation's goals/objectives are changing according to the situation", "I learn to increase my performance by observing others (change Agents)", "Are there any such change agents from whom you can learn in your organization", "Founder's background like age, Education, domicile, experience and affiliation are important for the success of the organization", "The organisation is surviving because it takes its employees into confidence in decision making", the employees of both DDS and MVF were in agreement to the degree of about 85% and 15% of disagreement. It could be inferred that in both the organizations we could observe elements of similarity on issues of Change Management.

Human Capital Management

On the statements pertaining to Human Capital Management, the employees of MVF were in complete agreement, where as employees of DDS were in agreement to varying degrees. The responses to the statements "Management of resources is the root cause for the success of organization", "Delegation and Decentralisation is essential for the success of any organization", were comparable in both the organizations with a degree of agreement about 89%, indicating that they held similar opinion about the statements on a majority scale. But with regard to the statement" Human Capital is more important than Social and Financial Capital for the success of the organization", it could be seen that 87% of MVF employees were in agreement with the statement, where as only 58% of DDS employees were in agreement. It could be inferred that majority employees of MVF felt human capital is more important, where as nearly 42% of DDS employees felt otherwise.

Tools of Change Management

With regard to the Tools of Change Management, it could be seen from Table 6.1, that the order of preference given by the respondents in DDS were different from that of MVF. When the researcher enquired the areas in which they want to be trained for coping with changing situation and growing demands from managements, the respondents had evinced interest in different areas of training, but on different priorities. The analysis showed that the employees of DDS preferred areas like Organization Management, Leadership Activities, Knowledge of Interventions, as their first preference, Group Dynamics, Role and Goal Clarity, Reporting Relationships and Personality Development as their second preference, Problem Solving, Communication Skills, Interpersonal Relations, Advocacy and Buy-in Skills as their third preference, Personality Development, Interpersonal Relations, Negotiation and Contracting Skills and Systems thinking and Understanding as the 4th preference and Coping Skills, Conflict Management, Stress Management and Motivation as the 5th preference. It was observed that some topics were repeatedly chosen as different preferences.

It could be seen from Table 6.1, that employees of MVF had chosen Communication Skills, Motivation, Leadership Activities and Group Dynamics as the 1st preference, Reporting Relationships, Conflict Management, Leadership Activities, Motivation as 2nd preference, Coping Skills, Role and Goal Clarity, Facilitation Skills and problem solving skills as the 3rd preference, Personality Development, Systems thinking and Understanding, Knowledge of Interventions and Negotiation and Contracting Skills as 4th preference, Advocacy and Buy-in Skills group Dynamics, Negotiation and Contracting Skills, Interpersonal Relations as 5th preference. There were some topics common to more than one preference given by the respondents of MVF.

The over all analysis of the responses given by employees of DDS and MVF indicated that in almost all areas, their perception was alike and in areas of difference also, the degree of disagreement was minimum or almost negligible. From the detailed analysis the researcher could conclude on some issues and give the findings and recommendations which are as followed.

The researcher has taken into consideration both qualitative and quantitative data obtained during the discussions with managements of CSOs as well as employees of both DDS and MVF alongside the primary data collected through the structured questionnaires. With the help of the information the researcher could collect the following findings, conclusions and recommendations were arrived at.

The research findings completely are in agreement with the hypothesis, which assumed that

(a) For service organizations like Civil Society Organisations systematic Human Resource Management practices are required.

Table 7.1: Cross Case Analysis on Tools of Change Management in DDS and MVF

S.No	*Tools of Change Management*	*Order of Preference*									
		1		*2*		*3*		*4*		*5*	
		DDS	*MVF*	*DDS*	*MVF*	*DDS*	*MVF*	*DDS*	*MVF*	*DDS*	*MVF*
1	Organisation Management	53	28	13	12	13	24	15	29	6	7
2	Role and goal clarity	27	20	39	29	15	30	14	18	5	3
3	Reporting relationships	9	17	37	38	21	8	6	12	27	25
4	Motivation	4	35	31	32	17	24	7	5	41	4
5	Leadership activities	45	33	24	32	17	21	9	8	5	6
6	Communication skills	21	45	33	8	29	12	7	30	10	5
7	Inter personal relations	8	30	29	10	24	18	36	10	3	32
8	Group Dynamics	17	31	44	3	7	15	10	12	22	39
9	Conflict Management	24	29	29	33	7	20	8	12	32	6
10	Stress Management	21	20	14	34	19	9	16	13	30	24
11	Personality Development	11	26	34	19	14	15	36	35	5	5
12	Facilitation Skills	40	12	27	8	14	29	14	21	5	30
13	Systems thinking and understanding	16	28	29	10	16	14	32	32	7	16
14	Problem solving skills	13	10	27	16	33	28	16	17	11	29
15	Knowledge of interventions	39	16	19	17	22	24	10	32	10	11
16	Advocacy / Buy-in skills	18	9	32	24	23	11	18	17	9	39
17	Negotiation / contracting skills	25	21	21	6	14	12	32	30	8	31
18	Coping skills	24	12	19	18	10	31	5	21	42	18

Notes: Figures indicated in the table are absolute number of responses of employees of DDS and MVF.

(b) With changing times and growing demands on the civil society organisations, they have to use Change Management Tools.

(c) Civil Society Organisations, like any other corporate inistitutions, need to take care of their Human Resources in order to sustain the changes.

Findings

On the whole, it infers that better HRM could be considered to facilitate the staff for self-development by creating an enabling environment, which would lead to better performance, and to grow along with the organization by reducing the turn over rate.

The analysis of internal management pertaining to governance or decision-making process, Human Resource Management, Gender relations and Financial Management has brought to light certain penetrating insights on CSO management practices. The decision making process in the selected organizations indicate understandably that the leader's role is conspicuous in all components of decision making process beginning with governance to conflicts among the staff. This manifests the ownership of the organization and commitment to the mission of the leaders.

The decentralization in the management could be noticed in the formation of different administrative and governing structures. The Human Resource Management discloses the proportion of staff at different levels and the reasons for turnover rate. It indicates that when there are optimum opportunities for self development of the staff through trainings the turn over rate will be low.

In particular, the motivational level of the junior staff in the CSOs tends to be very low because of cognitive dissonance. Most of the staff enter into development work by chance and continue to be there for a brief span and return to their consonant jobs as and when they are able to find one. Hence, the commitment, values and motivational level tend to be deplorably low.

Every organization must have means of ensuring role performance, replacing members who have migrated to the other jobs, coordinating subsystems, structure of authority, both of which arise out of organizational needs and are inseparable.

The primary target of organisational change tends to be the individual. It could be an individual's personality, the interpersonal relationship between members of peer groups, the norms of peer groups, the interpersonal relationship between members of the organizational family, the structure of a role, the role relationships of some segment of organizational space or the structure of the organization as a whole. It indicates that the change in individuals would bring about changes through additive principle in the organizational structure and conditions.

The management systems and practices in the CSOs have been analysed by looking at the decision-making process, Human Resource Management, Financial Management, and Gender Sensitivity in the selected organizations. In the decision making process, the leader's role is present either overtly or covertly in all the decisions. The core team also lends support to the leader in some of the major decisions. Most of the organizations have a minimum of two governance structures such as core team, staff team and the board. While the staff team's role is felt more in the intervention decisions such as planning, implementing and monitoring the activities, the core team involves itself in most of the decisions taken in the organization. The mega and support institutions tend to have highly competent members in the board, core team and staff members to plan their programmes professionally.

In the liaisoning, focus shift and financial decisions, the concurrence of the board is sought in all the organizations, which have the board as the supreme body.

In the staff appraisal and staff monitoring, the core team plays the support role to the leader. Most organizations have realized the relevance of having governance structures for decision-making. The prevalence of a highly competent board and core team also ensures better relations with the constituents and other secondary stakeholders to have robust strategic alliance.

Human Resource Management in the CSOs occupies a prime place because the staff takes it up as their first job or out of chance. In addition, the reward and incentive to the staff is not commensurate with the work unless they share the vision and mission of the organization. Hence, the opportunities for self-development through trainings only would provide an incentive for continuing the job for a longer duration.

Financial Management in the CSOs sector has been analysed through the funding details, expenditure pattern and opinion on the financial aspects from the leader. The funding details show that the foreign grants have been relatively low. Overall, only around 50 percent of the funding comes through foreign grants. Local funds and government grants have been on the rise.

Then expenditure pattern reveals that nearly three-fourth of the funds are allocated for salaries and project management. Only one fourth is spent on all other activities such as maintenance, trainings, infrastructure and corpus fund. This shows that the sustainability aspect has not been given adequate attention.

The Strategic Management is widely practiced in the CSO sector at present. In almost all the organizations, professional SWOT matrix is prepared to assess the opportunities and threats in the environment. This also facilitates in developing strategies for the organization. The SWOT matrix prepared out of the responses from the selected organizations and their strategies seem to coincide amazingly Though these questions were asked separately without giving any hint about the purpose for which it was taken, the results indicate that knowingly or unknowingly all the organizations practice powerful strategic planning. This SWOT analysis also gives the direction for future plans to the CSOs. In all these processes, the trainings have contributed remarkably.

Overall, the results show that trainings have contributed in bringing professionalism in the internal management of organizations by setting up sustainable structures and systems in the organizations. It has also helped to develop the personality and competency of staff by facilitating self-development. The self-development has led to reduction in the turnover rate in the organisation. The trainings also made the CSOs to realize the relevance of strategic alliances to become more effective in their intervention.

Conclusions

CSOs often fumble despite having an able leader and a dedicated staff because of poor Human Resource Management(HRM). HRM becomes an essential part of CSO Management, for, the majority of the staff takes up development work out of chance immediately after their education, as a stopgap arrangement. When they are fresh out of school or college or in their first job, they are not clear about their goals and about themselves. They do not know whether they work best in a big organization or a small one; whether they like working with people or working alone; whether they prosper in a situation of uncertainty or not; whether they need the pressure of deadlines to perform efficiently; whether they make decisions quickly or need to sleep on them. Hence it is the job of the leader or management to assess the stability of the person to a particular job, Since the staff on their own do not know about themselves, it lies on the management to find the suitable place to make him/her perform best.

Most of the staff does not continue to work for a CSO lest they share the vision of the organization. Particularly when they don't get paid adequately, they have to be compensated more out of opportunities for self-development. Self-development means acquiring both more capacity and also more weight as a person. By making people more responsible and accountable, the staff can be made to take a bigger view of themselves in terms of self-respect and self-confidence.

The CSO sector responds with its inherent spontaneity to emerging situations. It encountered decades of crisis, denial, opportunities and awakenings. Having faced rough weather for more than half a century, the sector has grown from marginality to become hope of the marginalised sections of society due to the state and market failure to address their problems. Realizing their failure to reach the marginalized sections of the society, both the state and market tend to rely on the CSO sector to provide public goods and services to the poor. Hence, the voluntary non-profit action is now treated as the third sector.

Thus, the CSOs are expected to play a responsible role in the ensuing situation. As the New Policy Agenda prescribes, the liberal economic and political policies also place tremendous hope on CSOs to carry forward the agenda through the millennium. Similarly, the victims of globalization and structural adjustment reforms also beseech the CSOs to come to their rescue. Thus, the millennium fixes a lot of responsibility on CSOs in providing a safety net from the spectral policies and reforms to the underprivileged and CSOs need a lot of change management to face the new challenges.

As the organizations grow in number and size, a higher degree of professionalism in the management and intervention is required to develop systems for the smooth flow of relevant information to run the organization. The number of organizations attending training on PME and Financial Management in addition to Strategic Management reflects the keen interest shown by CSOs for professionalism in their management. The demand for more professionalism facilitated the proliferation of support institutions, which prompted exchange of information in both vernacular and English Languages.

The structural adjustment programmes and the globalization policies in the post cold-war era have brought growing consensus on the role of CSOs in the development of marginalized people in the underdeveloped countries. The recognition of CSOs necessitates a mandate for the organization from an authentic constituency. This would be coming forth only when the organization has relevance, legitimacy and accountability. So the sustainability of an organization in the emerging development context rests on ensuring the three in the identity of the organization. This could be ascertained only through a highly professional systematic approach in managing the organization and external relations.

Managing the organization refers to establishing systems for governance, planning, monitoring and evaluation of both staff and intervention. In addition, it also necessitates a well-knit coordination between all these structures.

On the other hand, managing relations deals with the strategic alliances to harness the locally available opportunities and resources for bringing efficiency in the organization effectiveness in the intervention. It requires a healthy relationship with the government, market forces, civil society actors in the environment and the people. In this process, capacity building to promote professionalism within the organization becomes essential.

The governance, Human Resource Management and Financial Management have been quite systematic in most of the organizations. The planning, monitoring and evaluation systems have also been set up in majority of organizations. This indicates that most of the organizations have developed comprehensive structures to make the intervention and organization more effective. Better Human Resource Management and governance assists in reducing the turnover rate of staff, which is one of the serious problems faced by

CSOs through optimum opportunities for self-development and job security.

The reduction in value and ego conflicts in the organizations also brings down the dissatisfaction in the job. The dissatisfaction and lack of scope for growth in the job are the contributing factors for higher turnover. Better HRM only can help to promote team spirit and performance to accomplish the mission effectively.

Wherever the intensity of training was high, the impact is evidently remarkable. This also connotes that organizations have to devote more attention on promoting self-development of staff through capacity building exercise which has multi-faceted outcomes such as increase in professionalism, developing systems in the organization, and above all, the reduction in the turnover rate. The trainings have intensified the growth of organization in a symmetric way by developing systems to cope with the ensuing international development situation.

The SWOT analysis lends credence to the claim of their potential and opportunities in the environment. The strategies formulated through the scientific analysis of their capacities and the environment get the mandate of the authentic database. Hence, the implementation of strategies becomes successful. This analysis also provides ample scope for future planning. The results of SWOT analysis and future plans indicate that there is a systematic link between the two. Though most of the organizations do not practice it systematically, they arrive at it through intuition and perceptions. It could be still more effective, if it were done systematically.

Thus, the CSOs have inherent spontaneity to raise to the occasion, particularly where their services are needed and where there is opportunity for their sustainability. The CSOs bank more on perception, reality and intuition to acquire insights, knowledge and self-actualisation. The changing international development cooperation has forced the CSO sector to become more professional and organized to have identity, relevance, legitimacy and accountability.

The pace at which changes are taking place in the external environment needs to be matched by an internal mechanism within organizations that can interpret the impact of the change on the strategies and programmes of the CSO.

Since CSOs work with a social mission and there are several actors engaged in this mission, it is absolutely essential for them to be skillful in 'Boundary Management' and perceive the relatedness of an organization's mission to the larger 'Social Mission' and look for 'Alliance' and 'Synergy' levels with other "Key factors' in the larger environment . Therefore, strategic change management within the organization to maintain the social relevance of its mission and strategy becomes the crux of Human Resource Management within the CSO sector.

Recommendations

CSOs also face leadership problems. As the CSOs expands the area and scope of its activities, some prominent personalities often begin to assume overriding powers in running the organization. Taking initiative and making decisions become the prerogative of a few at the top. This increasing centralization affects flexibility of functioning, hampers democratization of decision making and obstructs the growth of new leaders.

The views and concerns of younger members of the organization are often overlooked, even suppressed. This gives way to groupism within the organization. Quite a few CSOs suffer from the absence of a second line of leadership. The process of decision making and style of functioning do not indicate a plan to build leaders and to include healthy organizational norms.

Poor maintenance of records and accounts and lack of attention to organization building through motivation, staff development and guidance are other problems. Most voluntary organizations lack the administrative and technical competence to prepare project proposals and apply for grants. This issue needs to be addressed immediately through training and capacity building among the staff of CSOs.

A low salary structure and inability to provide a career ladder limits the ability of CSOs to recruit and retain qualified and trained staff needed for several types of activities. Paid workers of CSOs often have a mixed set of attitudes. Some are genuinely interested and committed while others perceive this as an interim arrangement till a better alternative emerges. The absence of a career ladder results in a larger turnover. This naturally tends to affect the functioning of the CSOs.

CSOs must make a conscious effort to improve their own organizational structures and administrative competence including accounts and housekeeping. They must develop competence not only in problem solving and prompting development but also in motivating and sensitizing people and building capacity of the community for problem solving and sustainable development.

There must be greater co-ordination among CSO's and other Village Organisations to avoid duplication of services. A Coordinating Council of Civil Society Organisations will be useful for providing a forum for collaboration and co-operation and in jointly taking up issues of concern with the government.

A clear training policy must be implemented by CSOs as motivation is not enough. A professional approach is always able to achieve better results. Honorary workers, too, need training.

The larger CSOs should appropriate personnel policies for the staff. Programmes of CSOs must be documented and widely disseminated so that society is in better position to assess their endeavours. This would also serve as resource material for the others.

Most of the CSOs do not follow proper recruitment procedures. This effects their functioning. For recruitment to be effective, it is necessary to frame the recruitment rules setting out the qualifications, mode of recruitment, scale of pay, etc.

A job description also starts with the screening of applications, short listing the candidates, conducting a written test if necessary, consulting a selection committee, interviewing candidates and making the appointments. Usually a panel of names is drawn up in order of merit and appointment letters are sent accordingly.

Performance appraisal is the systematic assessment of the strengths and weaknesses of an employee's performance of assigned tasks during a specified period. It usually takes into account factors such as knowledge, undertaking, skills, achievements initiative, ability to relate to other persons in the organization, and to the clients, etc. Performance appraisal helps the agency to improve efficiency and to identify in an objective way employees who do better than others.

Training is now recognized as an investment in staff development. It not only increases knowledge, understanding and skills, but also provides better motivation. CSO agencies are now called upon to implement a wide range of programmes and engage in some degree of social engineering as well. Workers have constantly to interact with people, communicate with them and function as change agents.

Training helps not only in career development and efficiency of the employees, but also improves the agency's performance. Before conducting any training programme for the staff, careful planning of syllabus, resource persons, duration of training and the learning outcomes are important. A number of innovative training methodologies are now available which use a participatory multi-media approach.

Actions Recommended for Effective Change Management in CSOs

The following action points may be attempted by managements of CSOs for better Change Management in their respective organizations to cope with the future challenges.

1. Creation of employee friendly environment and regarding employees as valuable resources, worthy of receiving education and training throughout their career.
2. The managements should consider the views of employees in the organization and conduct periodic surveys to measure the employee satisfaction
3. Managements should reward superior performance with high responsibility jobs and promotional opportunities, as also, facilitating outstanding performers during annual day and other occasions.
4. The top management should ensure job rotation helping employee development and see that managers counsel subordinates for performance improvement and also to ensure managers take performance appraisals seriously.
5. The managements of CSOs should implement organisational welfare programmes ensuring the well being of employees.
6. Due importance should be given to grass root level workers training, while choosing qualitative programmes for external training, which should ultimately contribute to improvement of productivity and quality.
7. The management should introduce participatory appraisal system facilitating growth and learning by employees and a training system contributing to multi-skilling and contribution to improvement of productivity and quality service

8. The appraisal data should be used as input for recognition and encouragement of high performers and also keep the grievance redress machinery to be in place.
9. Management should be proactive in addressing the concerns of the employees and ensure optimum utilization of HR competencies.
10. It is suggested to emphasise on training on group dynamics and HR skills and the appraisal system should be so designed to distinguish the performers and non-performers.
11. Employees should be facilitated for innovative thinking and adequate resources for training should made available, which should result in developing managerial capability and HR skills.
12. The management should give importance to customer related matters and make decisions on facts and data.
13. Management should create awareness among employees about organizational vision, mission and goals and ensure well defined organizational structure and delegation of authority.
14. Feedback for improvement should be welcome from the employees and Promote quality service as an organizational value.
15. Employees should have belief in competence of Human Resources to meet any challenges and maintain cordial relations between organization and the community around.
16. Employee should be involved in community development programmes, ensuring high order team spirit, Interdependence and cohesive teams.
17. Management should monitor and evaluate strategic plans and create environment of openness and trust in the employees and value their opinions.

18. Empowerment of employees to solve problems should be facilitated and employees should be encouraged to contribute for quality improvement, through continuous dialogue between top management and programme implementation team.
19. The management should consider feedback from grass root level staff for making process improvements and also recognise operational efficiency and achievement in the organization.
20. Management should implement effective suggestion scheme and reward excellent suggestions.
21. Employees should be encouraged to report work related problems rather than routine matters.
22. The management should evaluate new projects before implementation and encourage employees to experiment with new methods and ideas.
23. It is the prime duty of the management of CSOs to reflect on concern for service in day to day operations.

Appendices

ANNEXURE I
QUESTIONNAIRE FOR MANAGEMENTS OF CSOs

Dear Sir / Madam,

We request you to kindly fill the following questionnaire and return the same through the self-addressed stamped envelope immediately so that we can analyse and interpret the data purely for academic purpose.

(To be filled up only by the Director / Secretary / Co-ordinator or any other person involved in Decision-Making or Management of the Organisation)

S.A. = Strongly Agree, A = Agree, M.A. = Moderately Agree, M.D.= Moderately Disagree, S.D. = Strongly Disagree

Personal Profile (G1)

1) Name of the Organisation :

2) Year of Establishment :

3) Background of the Founder : Educational / Social Service / Industrialist / Retired from Service / Others

4) Reference Group : **Gandhian:** Tribals, Dalits, Rural People **Socialist:** Women, Children, Youth

5) Ideology of the Organisation : Marxian / Gandhian /Socialist /Others

6) Do you have a Mission statement for the organisation : Yes / No

Organisational Objectives (G2)

7) Every organisation should have goals to function effectively : SA / A / MA / MD / SD

8) Every organisation should have objectives to achieve the goals: SA / A / MA / MD / SD

9) Functioning of the organisation depends on the motto with which we are working : SA / A / MA / MD / SD

10) We are working strictly in line with the objectives set out at the time of Incorporation of the organisation : SA / A / MA / MD / SD

11) Have you changed the activities over the period since inception : Yes / No

12) Organisational success depends on adapting to new challenges every time instead of a Consistency approach : SA / A / MA / MD / SD

13) Activities are mere activities. They should also be used as strategies to achieve the goals : SA / A / MA / MD / SD

14) **Internal Management: HRM (G3)**

Major Decision	*Centralised / Leader*	*Board of Governor*	*Core Committee*	*All Staff*	*Ad hoc Committee*	*Remark if any*

a) Planning of Activities

b) Implementation process for activities

c) Major Focus Shift

d) Financial Decisions

e) Monitoring of Activities

f) Employee recruitment

g) Promotions of employees

h) Pay hike / Incentives to employees

i) Performance Appraisals

j) Staff Monitoring

k) Problem solving

l) Liaisoning and Promotional activities

Decision-making Process in the organisation (please tick the appropriate box):

Recruitment (G4)

15 Recruitment of employees in the organisation should be based on policies such as gender proportion, Caste proportion : SA / A / MA / MD / SD

16 Employees should be recruited based on Competency alone : SA / A / MA / MD / SD

17 Qualified Specialist staff are helpful for the organisation : SA / A / MA / MD / SD

18 Experienced Generalist staff are useful for the organisation : SA / A / MA / MD / SD

19) How do you recruit staff? Through

a) Advertisements b) Recruitment Consultants
c) Aspirants Approach d) Reference from others

e) Spotting, meet and directly inviting the people
f) Others

Motivation (G5)

20 Retaining Employees in the organisation is becoming difficult : SA / A / MA / MD / SD

21 We are remunerating the employees according to their Competency / Skills / Qualifications : SA / A / MA / MD / SD

22 Commitment of our staff to the cause is : High/Moderate/Below average/Low

ANNEXURE II

EMPLOYEE QUESTIONNAIRE

Please tick (✔) the appropriate box.
(S.A. = Strongly Agree, A = Agree, M.A. = Moderately Agree, M.D.= Moderately Disagree, S.D. = Strongly Disagree)

Personal Profile (G1)

1. Name :

2. Age Group:

   a) 20-30 b) 30-40 c) 40-50 d) above 50

3. No. of Years of Experience:

   a) <5 b) 5-10 c) 10-15 d) above 15

4. Experience in the Present organisation (years):

   a) 1-4 b) 5-8 c) 9-12 d) above 12

5. Educational Qualifications:

   a) Below Graduation
   b) Graduate (BA/BCom/BSc)
   c) Post Graduate (MA/MCom/MSc)
   d) Professional Degree

6. Marital Status : Married / Unmarried

7. Area of Specialisation:
   a) Administration
   b) Field Activities
   c) Financial Management
   d) Capacity Building
   e) Policy Advocacy

8. Is this the first CSO you are working with: Yes/No

9. Did you know any thing about this organisation before joining this : Yes / No

10. How did you get recruited in this Organisation:
    a) Through Advertisement
    b) Reference
    c) Manpower consultancy
    d) Direct Approach
    e) Invitation from Management
    f) Experience in the present organisation
    g) Age

11. What prompted you to join this organisation:
    a) Need for job
    b) Interest in Social Service
    c) Persuasion from a friend
    d) Motivated by the work they are doing

12. What is the most important thing you look for from the organisation:
    a) Commitment of the management
    b) Salaries and benefits
    c) Service rendered to the poor
    d) Functional freedom

13. Did you observe any shift in the focus areas Yes/No during the last 5-10 years:

Employee Motivation (G2)

14. Service motto of the organisation motivates me to work in this organisation:
    SA A MA MD SD

15. The organisation should expand the activities to various Geographical locations in the State/Country:

    SA A MA MD SD

16. Monetary benefits alone motivate me to work in this organisation: SA A MA MD SD

17. Job satisfaction is important for me :
    SA A MA MD SD

18. Strong and committed leadership motivates employees in the organisation: SA A MA MD SD

Recruitment & Training (G3)

19. Employees should be recruited based on competency alone:
    SA A MA MD SD

20. Educational qualification alone is sufficient for better performance in a CSO:

    SA A MA MD SD

21. Training in motivation is essential for every employee:
    SA A MA MD SD

22. For improving the performance on the job, training is compulsory: SA A MA MD SD

Change Management (G4)

23. I am ready to take up the task/assignment given to me by my management immediately:

    SA A MA MD SD

24. My organisation's goals/objectives are changing according to the situation:
    SA A MA MD SD

25. I learn to increase my performance by observing others (change Agents): SA A MA MD SD

26. Are there any such change agents from whom you can learn in your organisation:
SA A MA MD SD

27. Founder's background like age, education, domicile, experience and affiliation are important for the success of the organisation:

SA A MA MD SD

28. The organisation is surviving because it takes its employees into confidence in decision-making:
SA A MA MD SD

Human Capital Management (G5)

29. Management of resources is the root cause for the success of organisation:

SA A MA MD SD

30. Human Capital is more important than Social and Financial Capital for the success of the organisation:

SA A MA MD SD

31. Delegation and Decentralisation is essential for the success of any organisation:
SA A MA MD SD

32. If changes have to be made in your organisation, which area would you like to initiate:
a) Working style
b) Reporting system
c) Procedures
d) Performance measurement & review
e). Training and development

33. I want to work in this organisation even if there are changes in Policy, leadership and management style: YES / NO

35. Coping with changing situation and growing demands from management,

    I want to be trained in (Please give your order of preference on 1 to 5 scale)

Tools of Change Management (G6)

Topic	*Order of Preference(1 to 5)*				
a) Organisation Management	1	2	3	4	5
b) Role and goal clarity	1	2	3	4	5
c) Reporting relationships	1	2	3	4	5
d) Motivation	1	2	3	4	5
e) Leadership activities	1	2	3	4	5
f) Communication skills	1	2	3	4	5
g) Inter-personal relations	1	2	3	4	5
h) Group dynamics	1	2	3	4	5
i) Conflict Management	1	2	3	4	5
j) Stress Management	1	2	3	4	5
k) Personality Development	1	2	3	4	5
l) Facilitation Skills	1	2	3	4	5
m) Systems thinking and understanding	1	2	3	4	5
n) Problem solving skills	1	2	3	4	5
o) Knowledge of interventions	1	2	3	4	5
p) Advocacy / Buy-in skills	1	2	3	4	5
q) Negotiation / contracting skills	1	2	3	4	5
r) Coping skills	1	2	3	4	5

ANNEXURE III

List of Civil Society Organisatons who responded to the questionnaire

1. *A.P. Urban And Rural Social Development Society* Ramachandra Pet, Chanakyapuri Colony,District: West Godavari
2. *Action For Integrated Development (AID)* H. No. 4-75, U.P.S. Street, Kalloor, District: Khammam
3. *ASSIST* G.t. Road, Chilakaluripet, District: Guntur
4. *AVAGAHANA* 22-12-13, Eluru Bazar, Guntur, District: Guntur
5. *AWARD* 1-3-151/1, Shastri Nagar, Mandal Nirmal, District: Adilabad
6. *Abhudaya Khadi Gramina Vikas Sangahm* D.no.2/125, Ramanpet, Attili District: West Goadavari
7. *Abhudhaya Mahila Mandali* 14th ward, Aminapet, Eluru, District: West Godavari
8. *Abhudhaya Mahila Mandali, Guntur* Dariya Nagar, opp. A.C. College, District: Guntur
9. *Academy of Gandhian Studies (AGS)* 2-2-1133/5/5, New Nallakunta District: Hyderabad
10. *Action Collective of Outcastes and Oppressed* 1-62, Gramasiri, Chikalapally, District: Medak
11. *Action Rural Technology and Service* (ARTS) Chandrayya Pet Street,Amudalavalasa District: Srikakulam

12. *Adarsh Mahila Mandali,* Hyderabad 2-2-185/39, Near Ayyappa Temple, Ramakrishna Nagar, District: Hyderabad

13. *Adarsha Mahila Mandali, Karimnagar (AMM)* Village Shayampet, Mandal – Jamikunta, District: Karimnagar

14. *Adarsh Mahila Mandali, Nizamabad (AMM)* Satyanarayan Puram,Near Bus Stop – Vemi, District: Nizamabad

15. *Adarsh Mahila Mandali (AMM)* H.No.9-3-627, Mohinipur, Siddipet District: Medak

16. *Adarsha Rural Development Society (ARDS)* H.No.17-1-120/A, Dugumallivari Street,Bapatla, District: Guntur

17. *Adarsha Seva Samithi* 4–1-14, Kothur Street, Hanamkonda, District: Warangal

18. *Adoni Area Rural Development Initiative Programme (AARDIP)* No.258, Mig-Ii,Housing Board Colony, Adoni, District: Kurnool

19. *Advance Rural Technology Hyderabad Inputs Centre (ARTHIC)* 52, Jagadish Nagar Colony, 1-35-341, Rasoolpura, Secunderabad

20. *Advancing the Ministeries of The Gospel (AMG)* Amg India International, Chilakaluripet, GT.Road, District: Guntur

21. *Ananda Mahila Mandali* H.No.2-73, 4th Floor,Chevella Mandal, District: Hyderabad

22. *Andrha Mahila Sabha* Andhra Mahila Sabha Building, University Road, Vidyanagar, Hyderabad

23. *Andhra Pradesh Natural History Society* 11-2-6, Das Palla Hills, District: Visakhapatnam

24. *Andhra Pradesh Rural Reconstruction Mission (APRRM)* 1-69, Cross Roads, Piler, District: Chittoor

25. *Andhra Pradesh Social Service Centre (APPSC)* Xavier Nagar, Ekeru, District: West Godavari

26. *Andhra Yuvati Mandali* H.No.50-3-4-769-4, Barkatpura, District: Hyderabad

27. *Anupama Women's Welfare Society* 2-1-407, Smruthi Bhavan,Nallakonta, Near Tilak Nagar Bridge, District: Hyderabad

28. *Arthik Samata Mandal (ASM)* Nastik Kendiram, Patamata, Near Benz Circle, District: Vijayawada

29. *Arundhathi Mahila Mandali (AMM)* D.No.7-17-363, Mallikharjunapet Guntur, District: Guntur

30. *Asmita Resource Centre For Women* Flat no.201, Padma Mohan Apartment, Street 6, Teachers Colony, Sec-Bad,

31. *Association for Research and Action on Rural & Tribal People* H.No.2-5-230, Nakkalagutta, Hanumkonda District: Warangal

32. *Association for Rural & Tribal Development* (ACTION) Krishna sadan, po Hukumpet, , Dr. Meda ranga Prasada Rao Gardens, Rajahmundry

33. *Association for Rural Involvement and Social Education (ARISE)* 7-15-26, 3rd Lane Street,Subbaiedo Nagar, Randapet, Rajahmundry

34. *Association for The Care Of The Aged* Door No.8-14-1, Red Cross Street, Gandhi Nagar, Kakinada,District: East Godavari

35. *Bapuji Rural Enlightment and Development Society*

(BREADS) Village & P.O Dimli,Via Niragam, Mandalam – Kotturu District: Srikakulam

36. *Bharati Nilayam Mahila Mandali* H.no.5-17, Near kumari veedi,p.o. Patancheru, Sangareddy, District: Medak

37. *Blood Donor's Organisaton for Social Service (BOSS)* 7-46, Vasavi nagar, MR. palli, Tirupati, District: Chittoor

38. *Blue Cross Of Hyderabad (BCH)* 8-2-269/10, Road 10, Banjara Hills, District: Hyderabad

39. *BOARD* 6-67, Road no. 1. Brindavan Colony, District: Hyderabad

40. *Centre for Integrated Rural Development (CIRD)* 7-1-995, Shankar Street, Monda Market, Secunderabad

41. *Chaitanya Rural Development Association* (CRDA) D.No.10-3-70, Gouthami Nagar, Kovour District: West Godavari

42. *Child Guidance Centre (CGC)* 8-13, Nehru Nagar, Ramanthapur District: Hyderabad

43. *Chittoor Rural Development Society (CRDS)* 6-8-918, Srinivasa Nagar, Ngo's Colony, K.T. Road, Tirupati

44. *Christian Action in Rural Development (CARD)* 17-5-18, Baptist Nagar, Kolanda Reddy, Vijayawada

45. *Christian Association for Medical Mission & People's Development* P.O.Box No.7, Samtha Nagar, Gbc Road, Ponnur District: Guntur

46. *Christian Concern Mission (CCM)* P.o. Bag no.5, Shamshabad, District: Ranga Reddy

47. *Christian Institute for Social Development (CISD)* Kattevaram, Mandal – Tenali, District: Guntur

48. *Citizens Against Pollution (CAP)* H.No.1-9-633, Vidya Nagar, District : Hyderabad

49. *Collective Order for Rural Reconstruction Education* (CORE) 14-145-14, Om Shakti Layout, Palace Extension, Kuppam District: Chittoor

50. *Collective Rural Development in India* (CRDI) 40-A, Electronic complex, ECIL P.O. District: Hyderabad

51. *Collective Rural Operations of The Poor* (CROP) Opp:Chandrashekhar Rice Mill, Mallevonigudem Road, Parigi,District: Ranga Reddy

52. *Community Awareness and Village Improvement* (CAVI) Kuchulnapally, Ipur Post and Mandal, District: Guntur

53. *Community And Rural Development Society* (CARDS) Santhosh Nagar, P.O.Box.No.309, District: Guntur

54. *Comprehensive Rural Development Society* (CRDS) D.No.11-8-11/6, Narsaraopet, Ramireddipet , District: Guntur

55. *Comprehensive Rural Operations Service Society* (CROSS) 1-69, Snehapuri, Nacharam District: Hyderabad

56. *Comprehensive Social Service Society* (CSSS) Vrikshamitra Bhavan, Yasoda Nagar, Pathapatnam, District: Srikakulam

57. *Confederation of A.P. Consumer Organisations* (CAPCO) 6-1-67/1/3, Lakdikapul, District: Hyderabad

58. *Constant Service in Developing Education and Rural Reconstruction* H. No. 3-309, V.l. Puram, Bapatla, District: Guntur

59. *Consumer Awareness and Research* (CARS) 6-1-67/1/3, Lakdikapul, District: Hyderabad

60. *Consumers Awareness Society (CAS)* 392-C, Tilak Road, Raseema Complex, Tirupati Districti : Chittoor

61. *Creative Organisation and Rural Development* (CORD) B.C. Colony, Narasipatnam District: Visakhapatnam

62. *Cuddapah District Harijan Grama Abhudaya Seva Samiti* (CDHGSS) 3-22, Jyoti Nagar, Badvel District: Cuddapah

63. *Cuddapah District Rural Development Society* Konkkarayapalli, Mandal-Chennur District: Cuddapah

64. *Cultural Action in Rural Development* (CARD) Nehru Nagar, Near Sudarshan Cinema, Pamidi District: Ananthapur

65. *Dalit Education and Economic Development Society* (DEEDS) Maniyanam palle, Dulikallu P.O., Denumur Mandal District: Chittoor

66. *Deccan Development Society (DDS)* 101, Krishna Residency,Street No 5, Begumpet, Hyderabad -560016

67. *Deepa Weaker Section Mahila Mandali* (DWSMM) 4-15-122/5, Bharatia Pet, 8th Lane District: Guntur

68. *Development Action of Women Network* (DAWN) D.No.7-6-332-2/a, Vengalarao Nagar, 3rd Lane District: Guntur

69. *Development Association For Women Needs* (DAWN) 4/607, Aravinda Nagar,R.T.C Bus, Stand, Back Side Siva Sankar Hospital District: Cuddapah

70. *Faith Action For Community Transformation* (FACT) 21/338/c, Bhaskara Puram, Machilipatnam District: Krishna

71. Forum Of Street Children Hyderabad (FSCH) 1-2-412/21, Domalguda, Opp. College Of Art, Science & Commerce District: Hyderabad

72. *Gandhi Kshetram Gandhi Kshetram*, Avani Gadda District: Krishna

73. *Gandhi Peace Centre (GPS)* 2-2-1133/5/6 A, New Nallakunta District: Hyderabad

74. *Gandhian United Action For Rural Development (GUARD)* Gandhi Kshetram, Avani Gadda District: Krishna

75. *Godavari delta Women Lace Coop. Cottage Industrial Society Ltd.* Rustumbada, Narasdur District: West Godavari

76. *Good Samritans Rural Development Society (GSRDS)* H.No.12-16-11, Daya Mansion, Gandhi Nagaram, Nidadavole,District: West Godavari

77. *Gospel for The Laymen And Organisation For The Rural Youth* P.O. Kondubhotlapalem, Baptla District: Guntur

78. *Gram Abhyudaya Mandali (GRAM)* Gram, Dhamaram District: Nizamabad

79. *Grama Abhyudaya Samstha (GAS)* Korrapad Road, Rajiv Gandhi Chowk, Prodatur District: Cuddapah

80. *Grama Naya Nirman Samiti (GNNS)* Jaya Prakash Nagar, Jammikhunta District: Karimnagar

81. *Grameena Vikas Samiti (GVS)* 6-8-947, Ngo's Colony, K.T. Road, Tirupati District: Chittoor

82. *Gramina Mahila Mandali (GMM)* Village Solipet, P.O. Cheekatimamidi, Mandal – B. Ramaram, District: Nalgonda

83 *Grow More Trees Association* 43-17-42, Sarvodaya Marg, Venkataraja Nagar District: Visakhapatnam

84. *Hands Of Compassion (HOC)* 15-12-40, Panasathota, Mandal – Narasaraopet District: Guntur

85. *Harijan Vyavasaya Karamik Sangham* (HVKS) Mandal – Amarhalur District: Guntur

86. *Hospitality Organisation & Uplift Preaching & Evangelism (HOPE)* Vidyanagar, Bapatla District: Guntur

87. *Ilahi Women's Association* (IWA) At jamikunta, p.o. Huzurabad taluq district: karimnagar

88. *Indira Mahila Mandali* 73-3-12/2, narayanpuram, Near Paper Mill, Kurnool Road, Rajahmundry

89. *Indira Sanghika Samkshema Mahila Mandali* D.no.6-17-67, 18/7 Arundal Pet ,Guntur District: Guntur

90. *Institute For Social Services (ISS)* 392, C, Tilak Road, Near Wine Shop, Tirupati District: Chittoor

91. *Institute of Resource Development And Social Management* (IRDAS) H.No.10-1-123/a/3/1, Saifabad District: Hyderabad

92. *Institute of Women And Child Welfare* (SAMKSHARMA) M.I.C 1683, Bhel, Ramachandrapuram,District: Medak

93. *Integrated Community Welfare Association* (ICWA) H.No.14-4-38(2), Jana Jagruti House, Pothuraju Mitta, P.O. Kandukur District: Prakasam

94. *Integrated Development Through Environmental Awakening (IDEA)* Flat no.4 c, Maharaja Towers, r.k. Mission road, District: Visakhapatnam

95. *Integrated Developmental Education Activate Society* (IDEAS) 6/122, Near Women & Child Welfare Office, Ravinder Nagar, District: Cuddapah

96. *Integrated Rural Community Development Society* (IRCDS) Village & P.O. Ravinder nagar, District: Cuddapah

97. *Integrated Rural Development Services* (IRDS) 32, Railway Colony, Picket, District: Hyderabad

98. *Integrity Rural And Tribal Development Society* (IRTDS) D.No.5-98-57/5, Becker Compound, Brodipet, District: Guntur

99. *Jagruthi* H.No.11-3-34/2, Nehru Nagar,District: Khammam

100. *Jagadamba Mahila Mandali Village Beggi,* Near Temple, Mandal – Komarade District: Vizianagaram

101. *Jana Chaitanya Samithi (JCS)* Post & Mandal, Pedakurapadu, District : Guntur

102. *Jawahar Urban And Rural Development Society* (JURDS) H.No.12/632, Near Jai Manamma, Kalyana Mantapam, Jesus Nagar ,District: Ananthapur

103. *Jeevan Jyoti Social Service Society* D.No.4-5-32/12, 1st Lane, Vidyanagar, District: Guntur

104. *Jeevana Jyoti Seva Sangham* Kasabgalli – Bharat Road, Kamareddy , District: Nizamabad

105. *Jyothi Weaker Section Mahila Mandal* (JWSMM) VILLAGE & P.O. Gorantala ,District: Guntur

106. *Kamala Nehru Mahila Mandali* Basweswara Street, Zaheerabad, District: Medak

107. *Kamala Nehru Mahila Mandali,* Chellapuram Village & P.O Chellapuram, Mandal – Dubbak, District: Medak

108. *Kanaka Durga Mahila Mandali* Village Maryamchalka, Mandal – Kasarajipili,District: Nalgonda

109. *Kanakadurga Rural Development Society* (KRDS) D.No.4-15-115, 8th lane,bharathpeta, opp. Cancer Hospital, District: Guntur

110. *Kasturba Mahila Mandali (KMM)* H.No.4-11, Amdapur Village,Mandal – Bodhan, District: Nizamabad

111. *Kolleru Rural Development Service Organisation* H.No.13-67/2, Akividu,Mediwada, District: West Godavari.

112. *Kotha Peta Mahila Mandali* Poturajawari Chowk, Kotta Peta ,District: Guntur

113. *Lebenshilfe* Municipal community hall, opp. Appu ghar, Mvp Colony,District: Visakhapatnam

114. *Lepra – India* P.B. No.1518, Krishnapuri Colony, West Maredpally, Secunderabad

115. *Legal Education Awareness & Rural Development Society (LEARDS)* Post & Mandal – Pedakurapadu, District: Guntur

116. *Light Organisation For Rural Development (LORD)* Nehru Centre, P.O & Mandal – Kainchikacherla, District: Krishna

117. *Literacy, Agriculture And Medical Project For Rural Development* Church Compound, Christian Pet, Taluk – Sattenapalli, District: Guntur

118. *Lurdumatha Mahila Samkshema* (LMS) Block Dharmaram, Mandal – Dichpally, District: Nizamabad

119. *M. Venkatarangaiah Foundation* (MVF) 28 Road No.1, Narayana Apartemnets#201,West Maredpally,Near East Maredpally, Secunderabad

120. *Mahalaxmi Welfare Society* D.No.05-08-10, DAKKINI STREET, DISTRICT: VIZIANAGARAM

121. *Maharshi Samba Murthy Institute of Social & Development Studies* 8-22-11, Datewari Street, Gandhi Nagar, Kakinada,District: East Godavari

122. *Mahila Abhyudaya Samstha (MAS)* 9, MIGH, Mehdipatnam, District: Hyderabad

123. *Mahila Sankshem Sangh (MASS)* 3-2-21, Thilak Nagar, Peddapally,District: Karimnagar

124. *Mallikarjuna Weaker Section Development Society (MWSDS)* Near Tuluka Office, Brodi Pet Main Road, Brodipet, District: Guntur

125. *Manasika Vikas Kendram* D.No.23-16-17, Purushottam Street,Park Road, Satyanarayanapuram,Vijayawada

126. *Manu Centre* 2-2-647/185/14, Sharada Nagar, Plot No.19, Street No.2, Bagh Amberpet,District: Hyderabad

127. *Margadarsi* 1-29, Jayaprakash Road,Newpet, Kuppam, District: Chitoor

128. *Marsha Mahila Seva Sangham* H.No.1-3-125/2, Old Bazar, District: Karimnagar

129. *Mary Matha Mahila Mandali* P.O. & Mandal – Pedanandipadu, District: Guntur

130. *Mary Matha Weaker Sections Mahila Mandali* Post & Mandal – Muppalla, District: Guntur

131. *Mass Action Forest Range Officer Social Service Society (MASS)* Narasaraopet, District: Guntur

132. *Mass Education Movement* 14-122/2, Palace Road, Kuppam, District: Srikakulam

133. *Mayuri Mahila Mandali* H.No.18-7-670/1, Charinaka, Outside Gowlipura, District: Hyderabad

134. *Mercy Minority Educational Society (MMES)* D.No.13-580, 1st Cross,Ramachandranagar, District: Ananthapur

135. *Modern Architects For Rural India (MARI)* H.No.3-1-94, Kakatiya Colony,Opp. Alankar Theater, Hanam Konda,District: Warangal

136. *Nagarjuna Integrated Rural Development Society (NIRDS)* D.No.7-6-846/7A, Vivekananda Nagar, 1st Lane, Janmabhoomi Road,District: Guntur

137. *Nalgonda Diocese Social Service Society* Duppalapally Road, District: Nalgonda

138. *National Education Minorities Society* (NEMS) D.No.15-12-53, Surya Hanumaya Apartments, Kothapet, District: Guntur

139. *National Muslim Minorities And Backward Classes Welfare Association* D.No.14-2-204, Stadium Road,District : Guntur

140. *New Academy Of Tribal Upliftment And Enlightenment (NATURE)* H.No.2-10-717, Teacher's Colony, Waddepally, Hanamkonda, District: Warangal

141. *New Life Ministries (NLM)* 5-2, Panditavilluru, Via Maruteru, District: West Godavari

142. *Nirmala Harijana Girijana Seva Sadan* 8/33, Suguna Nilayam, R.S. Road, Kodur, District: Cuddapah

143. *Orphans Faith Home (BUILD)* Lakshmana Rao Puram, Machilipatnam, District : Krishna

144. *PART* 11-92, Rajiv Nagar, District: Adilabad

145. *PILUPU* Pilupu, Kishan Nagar, Mandal – Bhongir, District: Nalgonda

146. *Parkal Rural Development Centre* 1-8-571, Nikkalgutta, Opp:Water Tank, Hanumkonda,District: Warangal

147. *People Oriented Organisation For Reconstruction* (POOR) Vardarajulu Building, South Palace Road, Kuppam, District: Chittoor

148. *People's Action For Social Service (PASS)* 10-12, Maruthi Nagar, Tirupati, District: Chittoor

149. *People's Action In Development (PAID)* 3/1723, Zionpuram, Raja Reddy Street, District: Cuddapah

150. *People's Educational Society (PES)* H.No.3-1-45, Opp: Inspection Bungalow, District: Karimnagar

151. *People's Organisation For Development Action (*PODA) D.No.2-727/1, P.B.No.56, Shanti Nagar Colony, District: Chittoor

152. *People Action For Creative Educatin (PEACE)* Peace, Bhongir, District: Nalgonda

153. *Poor People's Development Society (PPDS)* D.No.2 b-28-118, 1st Lane, Netaji Nagar, At. Agraharam, District: Guntur

154. *Prabhavathi Weaker Section Mahila Mandali* D.No.7-17-322, 2nd Lane, Mallikarjunapet, District: Guntur

155. *Pragathi Charities Dargamitta,* Near T.B. Hospital,P.O. Box 14,District: Nellore

156. *Praja Abyudaya Seva Samiti (PASS)* Plot No.233, D.No.4-1899, Durga Nagar Colony, District: Chittoor

157. *Praja Shakti Vidya Sangham* Chaithanya nilayam, 8th ward,Avanigadda, District: Krishna

158. *Rural Development Social Service Society* (RDSSS) D.No.1/128, prakasam nagar,Yerraguntla R.S., District: Cuddapah

159. *Raghu Mahila Vikas* 2/1, Aundel Pet, Near Sher Mehal Cinema, District: Guntur

160. *Relief Organisation For Handicapped (ROH)* Sevamandir, Hindupur, District: Ananthapur

161. *Renuka Mahila Mandali* 5-45, ramnagar, Miriyalagudam, Mandal – Kesarajapalem, District: Nalgonda

162. *Research Integrated Social Development Action (RISDA)* D.no.3-581, Raja Reddy Street, Opp. Postal Colony, District: Cuddapah

163. *Rural Agriculture And Gramodyog Development Society* St. Mary's Hospital Complex,Pakka Banda, District: Khammam

164. *Rural Community Development Society* (RCDS) D.No.5/389, Ravinder Nagar, District: Cuddapah

165. *Rural Development Advisory Service (RDAS)* G-301, Ruhaina Apartments,12-13-1236, Tarnaka, Secunderabad

166. *Rural Development Organisation* (RDO) 6/42, Gadicheral Rama Rao Steet,District: Cuddapah

167. *Rural Development Society (RDS)* Bellalavari Street, Jammalamadugu, District: Cuddapah

168. *Rural Education Development Society* (REDS) P.o. Itah nagar, Tenali, District: Guntur

169. *Rural Health, Education, Agriculture & Development Society* 28-842, Kannaiah Naidu Colony,Backside Of Government Hospital,District: Chittoor

170. *Rural Institute For Development And Education* (RIDE) Garigachinne palli, V. Mittapalli Post, Kuppam, District: Chittoor

171. *Rural Institute For Social Education* (RISE) 6-8-1037, NGOS Colony,K.T. Road, Tirupati,District: Chittoor

172. *Rural Organisation Economic Education For Women* (ROSEE) D.No.1-1-8 B, Abdpet, Near RTC Bus Stand, Hindupur,District: Anathapur

173. *Rural Organisation For Social Education* (ROSE) D.No.19-3-2/64, Sreenivasapuram, Renigunta Road, Tirupati, District: Chittoor

174. *Rural Organisation For Social Emancipation* (ROSE) P.o. Kondapaturu, Mandal – Kakumanu, District: Guntur

175. *SADHANA, Secunderabad* H.No.19, Vijay Nagar Colony, Picket, District: Hyderabad

176. *SAHANIVASA* P.B.No.47, D.No.22-977-1, Moruganipalli Road, District: Chittoor

177. *SNEHA* 6-2-49, Karaji Colony, Hanamkonda, District: Warangal

178. *SPANDANA*, Guntur 5-62-3/1, 1st Lane, Pandari Puram, District: Guntur

179. *SWEEKAR* Upkar Circle, Picket, Secunderabad, District: Hyderabad

180. *Samata Mahila Mandali* 3rd Ward, Pallkol, District: West Godavari

181. *Samskar Organisation* Chelli Nilayam, Vami, District: Nizamabad

182. *Sanghamitra Service Society (SANGHAMITRA)* 74-14-52, Krishna Nagar, Vijayawada, District: Krishna

183. *Sanghika Vidya Samstha (SVS)* 19-8-75, f-1, Sivaji nagar, R.C. Road, Tirupati, District: Chittoor

184. *Sanjay Memorial Technical Educational Society (SMTES)* 10-475, Bazar Street, District Chittoor

185. *Saraswati Mahila Mandali (SMM)* AT. Kallupali, Manali – Veenavanka, District: Karimnagar

186. *Sarda Mahila Mandali* Village Kotagiri, Mandal – Kotagiri, District: Nizamabad

187. *Self Employed Women's Association (SEWA)* Lane No.3, Srinagar Colony, District: Guntur

188. *Seva Medical And Educational Society (SMDS)* D.No.6-12-27, 12/1, Arundel Pet, 12th Lane, District: Guntur

189. *Seva Sadan* 4th Lane, Vasantarayapuram,Arundal Pet Post , District: Guntur

190. *Siloam Leprosy And Rehabilitation Welfare Society (SLRWS)* 9/86, Lingeshwar Nagar, Near Bairagipattada, Tirupati, District: Chittoor

191. *Social Health Awareness And Rural Evangelism (SHARE)* Film Godow Street, Baptist Nagar, Vijayawada, District: Krishna

192. *Social, Educational And Economic Development Society* (SEEDS) P.B. No.249, D.No.7-17-199/3, 3rd Lane, Srinagar, District: Guntur

193. *Society For Health Awareness And Rural Education (SHARE)*P.O.Jagapuram, Mandal- Edlapadu, District: Guntur

194. *Society For Health*, Education And Development (SHED) Mission House, D.No.17-7-3, Karunapuram Street, Hindupur, District: Ananthapur

195. *Society For Integrated Development In Urban And Rural Areas* 144/2 RT, Vijayanagar Colony,District: Hyderabad

196. *Society For Non-Formal Education*, Health And Awareness (SNEHA) P.G. Bazar, Sathupally, District: Khammam

197. *Society For Rural Reconstruction and Development (SRRD)* 10-264-b, Gandhi Road, District: Chittoor

198. *Sree Durga Mahila Mandali* At/P.O. Pandali Paka, Near Santama Temple, Mandal – Bikkavolu, District: East Godavari

199. *St. Ann's Manovikas Kendra* Bharathpet, 7th Lane, Amaravathi Road, District: Guntur

200. *St. Mary's Polio Rehabilitation Centre* St. Mary's Polio Rehabilitation Centre, Khammam, District: Khammam

201. *Star Mahila Mandali(SMM)* H.no.5-2-295, At. Rahimpura, P.O. Korutla, District: Karimnagar

202. *Thakur Hariprasad Inst. Of Res. & Rehabilitation For Mentally Handicap* Vivekananda Nagar, Dilsuknagar, Hyderabad

203. *The Bharath Abhyudaya Seva Samithi (BASS)* P.O. Box 336, 7th Lane, Srinivasa Rao Thota ,District: Guntur

204. *The Catholic Health Association Of India (CHAI)* 157/6 Staff Road, Gun Rock Enclave, Secunderabad

205. *The Cuddapah District Khadigramabhyudaya Samastha* (CDKGS) D.No.11/397, Peeru Shab Street, District: Cuddapah

206. *The Leprosy Mission*: Comprehensive Health Care Unit Parvathipuram, District: Vizianagaram

207. *The Meerabai Weaker Section Mahila Mandali* (TMWSMM) Gopala Krishna Yandadi Tribal Colony, Arundelpet, 18th Lane,District: Guntur

208. *The Nurjahan Mahila Mandali (TNMM)* Old Police Colony, Back Side Super Bazar, AC College, Dariya Nagar,District: Guntur

209. *The Laxmi Raghu Ram Weaker Section Mahila Mandali* D.No.4-16-489, 8th Ward, Potti Sreeramulu Nagar, District: Guntur

210. Thinker's Society S.C.V.S. College, Post & Mandal Chilkaluripet, District: Guntur

211. *Uma Educational & Technical Society Manovikas Nagar*, Behind Teachers Colony, Kakinada, District: Kakinada

212. *Uma Mano Vikash Kendra Rayudupalcalu*, Kakinada, District: East Godavari

213. *Vimochana* D.No.28/12/2, Ambativari Street, Viajaywada,District: Krishna

214. *Valley of Love And Compassion (VLC)* Christian Colony, Amaravathi, District: Guntur

215. *Vasavya Mahila Mandali (VASAVYA)* Benz Circle, Vasavya Nagar, Vijayawada

216. *Vasavya Society For Rural Development (VASORD)* 104, Reliance Enclave, Venktaramana Colony, Khairatabad, District: Hyderabad

217. *Vedantha Mahila Mandali (VMM)* 4-1478, Bursaddu Mattam, Near Super Bazar Road, Proddatur, District: Cuddapah

218. *Venkata Ramana Mahila Mandali* D.No.5-71-33, 6/21, Brodipet, District: Guntur

219. *Venkateshwara Mahila Mandali (VMM)* 4-15-39, Bharatipeta, 5th Lane, Guntur,District: Guntur

220. *Venugopal Mahila* Mandali New Police Quarters, 4th Lane, Nagarampalem, District: Guntur

221. *Villages In Partnership* (VIP) 8-5-24, Teachers Colony, District: Mehboobnagar

222. *Vimukti Leprosy Relief Association* Beside R.T.C. Complex, Perrajupeta, Kakinada, District: East Godavari

223. *Vudayasree Mahila Mandali* D.No.5-78-18/1, 6/3 Pandaripuram, District: Guntur

224. *Vivekananda Educational Centre (VEC)* Desipally, P.O. Veenavanka, District: Karimnagar

225. *Warangal Cousumers Council* 2-5-360, Nakkalgutta, Hanumkonda, District: Warangal

Index

□□□